The Dryden
Interviews

The Dryden Interviews

Dialogues on the Psychotherapeutic Process

Windy Dryden

Whurr Publishers
London

First published 1992 by
Whurr Publishers Ltd
19b Compton Terrace, London N1 2UN, England

British Library Cataloguing in Publication Data

A catalogue record for this book
is available from the British Library

ISBN 1-870332-73-3

Photoset by Inforum, Rowlands Castle, Hants
Printed and bound in the United Kingdom by
Athenaeum Press Ltd, Newcastle upon Tyne

Preface

Counselling and psychotherapy are based on a dialogue between therapist and client and yet most books on the subject involve the writer in a one-way communication with the reader. One of my interests over the years has been to try and capture the flavour of a dialogue in various publications. In doing this I have published a variety of interviews in which I have engaged a number of counsellors and psychotherapists in discussion on a variety of different therapeutic topics. This interest emerged out of a discovery that informal discussions that I have had with writers on therapy often proved to be more revealing than a reading of these authors' works.

In this book I have sought to bring together a representative sample of my previously published interviews and, in addition, I have included six interviews conducted especially for this volume. Interview 1 was conducted with Albert Ellis for 'Lifelines', a series of articles with leading counsellors and therapists published in the *Journal of Counseling and Development*. This interview caused something of a stir in that certain profane words used by Ellis in the original interview were replaced with dashes by the journal, presumably to spare the sensitivities of some of its readers. A brief correspondence appeared in subsequent issues of the journal which concerned the pros and cons of this form of censorship. The interview appears here as it was published in the journal.

Interview 2 is taken from my first book of interviews, entitled *Therapists' Dilemmas*. This book was published in 1985 and contained discussions with 14 therapists on the dilemmas of therapeutic practice. I have chosen to include the interview with Peter Lomas here because it was the one that readers considered to be of most relevance to the dilemmas of their own practice.

Interview 3 is a dialogue that I had with Michael Barkham (published in the *Counselling Psychology Review*) on the two-plus-one model of brief intervention that he pioneered with colleagues at the MRC Social and

Applied Unit at Sheffield University, whilst interviews 4 and 5, with Andrew Swart and Jill Sinclair respectively, were prepared for publication in the *British Journal of Guidance and Counselling*, an established journal which at the end of the 1980s sought to introduce innovative sections of which a regular annual interview was one.

Interview 6 was taken from one of three volumes that were published in 1991 in a series entitled *Therapeutically Speaking*. Each volume in this series included several interviews that I conducted with a leading American figure in the field of counselling and psychotherapy. To date the series includes books of interviews with Albert Ellis, John Norcross and Arnold Lazarus. The interview I chose for inclusion in this volume is a very interesting discussion that I had with Arnold Lazarus on various dos and don'ts and sacred cows in psychotherapy.

As mentioned earlier, interviews 7–12 were especially conducted for inclusion in the present volume. Interview 7 explores John Cobb's experiences of being a therapist on the late-night counselling television programme called *A Problem Aired*, whilst interview 8 traces John Marzillier's development from a behaviour therapist to one whose growing interest is in the psychodynamic therapies. Interview 9 explores Pat Milner's experiences of being a counsellor with ME, whilst interview 10 gives John Rowan an opportunity to expand on his views regarding the importance of therapists working with the 'whole person' of their clients. In interview 11, Brian Thorne takes up a theme that John Rowan briefly alludes to in the previous interview, that of the place of spirituality in therapy – here with special reference to person-centred counselling. Finally, in interview 12, I explore with John and Marcia Davis the relationship between being married and their work as psychotherapists.

I saw my role as interviewer to be primarily facilitative, helping the interviewees to articulate their views and elaborate on them. I chose to intervene and ask questions about the implications of these views whenever I saw fit, and only occasionally did I seek to challenge my interviewees. I took the position that they were guests who were to be encouraged to explore their ideas rather than to be grilled on them.

After conducting an interview it would be transcribed. I would then work to improve English expression, while seeking to retain the colloquial nature of the dialogue. Then I sent the transcript to the interviewee and encouraged him or her to make changes as the person saw fit. Above all, I wanted all interviewees to feel that their views had been accurately represented.

I hope that you the reader will get as much pleasure and instruction from studying these interviews as I did from conducting them. Finally, I wish to thank all my interviewees for their enthusiastic participation.

Windy Dryden, London
April 1992

Contents

Acknowledgements

I wish to thank the following for giving me permission to reproduce previously published material in this book:

The American Association of Counseling and Development for the interview with Albert Ellis (previously published in the *Journal of Counseling and Development*, 1989, **67**, 539–546).

Open University Press for the interviews with Peter Lomas (previously published in W. Dryden (1985) *Therapists' Dilemmas*) and Arnold Lazarus (previously published in W. Dryden (1991) *A Dialogue with Arnold Lazarus: 'It Depends'*).

Hobsons Publishing for the interviews with Andrew Swart (previously published in the *British Journal of Guidance and Counselling*, 1990, **18**, 308–320) and Jill Sinclair (previously published in the *British Journal of Guidance and Counselling*, 1991, **19**, 320–332).

British Psychological Society Special Group in Counselling Psychology for the interview with Michael Barkham (previously published in *Counselling Psychology Review*, 1990, **5**(4), 5–18).

Chapter 1
An Efficient and Passionate Life

An Interview with Albert Ellis

There can be few professionals and students of counselling who are not familiar with the work and achievements of Albert Ellis. He has been rated as the second most influential psychotherapist by a sample selected from Division 12 (Clinical Psychology) and Division 17 (Counseling Psychology) of the American Psychological Association (Smith, 1982). His published work since 1957 has been most frequently cited in major counselling articles when compared to his contemporaries (Heesacker, Heppner and Rogers, 1982) in the fields of counselling and psychotherapy, and in 1985 he received the APA award for Distinguished Professional Contributions. His voluminous bibliography occupied 16 pages in the 1986 issue of the journal *American Psychologist*, in which his award was cited. He maintains to this day a very busy clinical practice, is involved heavily in training workshops and supervision activities, and undertakes many speaking engagements in North America and throughout the world. People can be forgiven for believing that there is a team of Albert Ellis clones working away on behalf of the Institute for Rational–Emotive Therapy, of which Ellis is executive director. But no, one man has achieved all this – a man blessed, as he claims, with a biological make-up suited to all this industry.

Ellis's professional contributions have already been the subject of a published interview in the *Personnel and Guidance Journal* (Weinrach, 1980), and so in the current interview I focus more on Albert Ellis, the man.

While preparing for this interview, I canvassed several of Ellis's professional colleagues concerning areas of his personal life that might hold the greatest interest for a professional readership. Four such areas emerged and form the basis for the interview. First, we discuss Ellis's early days. Here, Ellis places himself in his family context and sketches some of the early influences that encouraged him to pursue a career in psychotherapy. Secondly, we discuss the women in his life. Rumours abound about Ellis's sex and love life, and in this section Ellis puts the record straight concerning this important area of his life. Thirdly we discuss Ellis's personal characteristics. People who hear Ellis lecture often comment on his abrasive, humorous and flamboyant style. In this part of the interview Ellis discusses this point and outlines, more broadly, how he sees himself in terms of his personal attributes. Finally, we focus on Ellis's personal reflections on his professional career. Here, Ellis discusses his feelings about his professional career to date

1

and shares his hopes concerning how he would like to be remembered for his professional contributions.

It is perhaps fitting that this interview was conducted by a British counselling psychologist, as this attests to Ellis's international impact on the fields of counselling and psychotherapy.

Early Days

Windy Dryden: Can you tell me something of your early days?

Albert Ellis: Well, I was born in 1913 in Pittsburgh. I had a brother, 19 months younger than me, and a sister who was 4 years younger. To some degree ours was a family where people went their own way. My mother was a neglectful woman in her own nice way. She was gregarious and would spend a lot of time with her friends from the temple and the neighbourhood. As a result, I learned to take care of myself and, to a mild degree, of both my brother and sister, although my brother was also very independent. While my brother and I didn't mind this benign neglect because we could live our own lives and my mother was pleasant enough when she was around, my sister felt very deprived and would whine and scream about this deprivation. I do remember, however, that my mother used to comfort me when I got bad headaches, which happened fairly frequently in my childhood.

Windy Dryden: What was your father like?

Albert Ellis: He was rarely around, so I don't recall missing him that much whenever he was absent. When he was around, he was bright and charming and got on okay with my mother, although they later divorced when she discovered that he had been having an affair with her best friend. Basically, he didn't feature very much in my early days.

Windy Dryden: How did you get on with your brother and sister?

Albert Ellis: My brother was a rebel and would literally —— on the floor and do all kinds of messy things, like throwing spitballs in class. But we got on quite well. We were companions, shared common daydreams aloud together, and usually had common interests. At the beginning my sister was okay but [she] later became a real pain in the ass and was obnoxious, especially to my brother. They used to fight with one another, and I used to have to stop them from fighting. I didn't like my sister but made peace with her and sort of accepted her. However, I never used to upset myself about her bad behaviour. You could say that I was the favourite in the family since I was fairly nice and got along with my mother and my father, when he was around. I was not a rebel like my brother nor a complainer like my sister.

Windy Dryden: How did you react to your parents' divorce?

Albert Ellis: Well, they didn't tell us officially for a year after the divorce, but I found out about it at the time when I was age 12, having overheard a conversation between my mother and my aunt. I was somewhat surprised but not shocked about it. In fact, I was more surprised that they spoke about it in such a secretive way. I didn't take it badly nor did I miss my father since, as I've said, he was rarely around even when they were married.

Windy Dryden: Did anything adversely affect your childhood?

Albert Ellis: The main thing that was wrong with my childhood was that I got nephritis at the age of 4½ and almost died from an infected tonsil. Between the ages of 4½ and 9 I was in the hospital about nine times, usually for a short while, although once I was hospitalized for 10 months. This interrupted my schooling quite a bit, and for a time I was not allowed to engage in athletics with other children since I was considered to be re-cuperating. However, I was not unduly bothered about all these things. I was bothered about the severe headaches that I had regularly as a child. I think this experience contributed to my preoccupation with keeping in good health.

Windy Dryden: Looking back on your childhood now, can you see any signs that might account for the fact that you later pursued a career in psychotherapy?

Albert Ellis: I always seemed to have been the kind of person who, when unhappy, made an effort to think about and figure out ways to make myself less unhappy. In a way I was a born therapist for myself. It certainly came naturally to me. Later on, I used this problem-solving tendency to help my friends with their problems, but first I used it with myself.

Windy Dryden: What kind of things were you most upset about in your childhood?

Albert Ellis: Well, I used to be quite anxious. I used to worry sometimes if my mother was very late getting home from the temple or her bridge game. I was shy, first of authority figures – school principals, for example – and then with girls. But I was not afraid of what my parents thought of me or anything like that.

Women and Marriage

Windy Dryden: You mentioned being shy around girls. When did you start to overcome this anxiety?

Albert Ellis: Not until I was 19, when I forced myself to talk to a hundred girls in a row in the Bronx Botanical Gardens during the period of one month.

Windy Dryden: That's interesting. You spoke earlier of being a natural problem solver from an early age, and yet you didn't get over your anxiety about approaching women until much later. How do you account for that?

Albert Ellis: The answer is probably that until that time I was only cognitive in my problem solving and then forced myself to be behavioural. The only way you really get over shyness is by forcing yourself to act when you're uncomfortable.

Windy Dryden: What happened after you overcame your shyness with women?

Albert Ellis: From my early twenties and thereafter I related marvellously to women because I was interested in them and their problems. I've always preferred the company of women to men because in general they more easily talk intimately about themselves and their problems than men do, and I found that I could express my problem-solving tendencies with them as well as relate to them sexually. Indeed, I had one of the best records in New York City of getting women to bed – by listening and talking to them and not by immediately making passes.

Windy Dryden: You've been married and divorced twice and have been living now with the same woman for 24 years. Perhaps you could say a little about each of these relationships.

Albert Ellis: My first wife was named Karyl, and we got married in 1937. She had been seeing one of my ex-friends who was married and who had been lying to her. We both confronted him with his lies and thereafter I got to know her and fell in love with her very quickly. She was an actress, very bright and attractive, but had severe emotional problems. However, even her nuttiness attracted me in the beginning. She was very erratic, sometimes showing her love for me, while neglecting me at other times. I became very hung up on her but got over this while walking one night in the Bronx Botanical Gardens by proving to myself that I didn't need her. When I told her this and suggested breaking up, she foolishly suggested that we get married.

Windy Dryden: And you agreed?

Albert Ellis: I agreed experimentally. In fact, it was supposed to be a secret marriage, since her parents wanted her to marry a rich man who would take care of them. However, she told them of our plans and, even though this created havoc, told them again after we got married. On discovering this on the night of our wedding, I decided then and there to divorce her because I realised that she couldn't be trusted. She immediately got involved with a very erratic guy who left her, and I helped to talk her out of a mental breakdown over this. After our annulment came through, we started living together and stayed together for a year, during which time she was as batty as she could be.

Windy Dryden: Do you regret this episode?

Albert Ellis: No, I thought it was a great learning experience. I learned not to live with a woman who was that crazy.

Windy Dryden: What happened then?

Albert Ellis: I went with a number of women but no one special until I met Gertrude, with whom I had the greatest romance in human history for 4 years and whom I almost married twice. I didn't marry her because, first, she wouldn't agree to our living in an apartment with at least one separate room where I could focus on my work free from interruption and, second, she was too gregarious for me. She wanted literally to have three dinner parties a week after we got married and, as that would take up far too much of my time, we agreed to disagree and she married someone else.

Windy Dryden: What was your second marriage like?

Albert Ellis: I married Rhoda in 1956. She was a dancer, also bright and attractive, but far more sensible than Karyl. At first, things were fine because her busy schedule matched my busy schedule. But then she hurt her foot and couldn't dance that much. She wanted me to spend more time with her and her dancer friends, who were not to my taste, and things started to go badly between us. Finally, we decided to divorce after being married for 2 years.

Windy Dryden: Did you stay friendly with her?

Albert Ellis: I've stayed friendly with both my ex-wives. Rhoda has even given some workshops at the Institute for Rational–Emotive Therapy.

Windy Dryden: So you got divorced in 1958 and met your current partner, Janet Wolfe, in 1964 when she was age 24, and that relationship has lasted 24 years and is still going strong. Why do you think this relationship has lasted while the others did not?

Albert Ellis: Well, Janet is not only bright and attractive, as the others were, but she really is much better for me. Emotionally, we have a solid relationship where we like and love each other and where we do not need the superromantic attachment that was there in the beginning. Janet really is solid in the sense that she helped me build the Institute for Rational–Emotive Therapy and does her own work here. Janet is the one woman in my life with whom I've been able to have quality time rather than quantity time. The others would get upset after a while when there was not enough quantity time. Janet, on the other hand, is into her own work and has her own friends, and the arrangement seems to suit both of us quite well.

Windy Dryden: Is it a monogamous relationship?

Albert Ellis: It tends to be so now, although in the past we have had an open relationship where we both have had affairs. But none of these has seriously threatened our relationship.

Windy Dryden: You don't have any children. Has that been a conscious decision?

Albert Ellis: Oh yes, a very conscious decision. There's no possibility of my having children now, since in 1972 I had a prostate operation, including sterilisation to make it safer, but before that it was a conscious decision.

Windy Dryden: Why was that?

Albert Ellis: Well, from my side, I would not have had children as I would not have been an adequate father to any child. I would not have been prepared to spend time taking the kid to baseball games or to do any of the normal things that people do with children. It would have been interesting for me to have been a father and to see how my children would have developed, but as I would not have spent that much time with them due to my work, then that would have been unfair to the children. Incidentally, Janet agrees with my position on this.

Windy Dryden: In terms of your relationships with women, what seems to be important to you is to have a relationship where you can devote a major proportion of your life to your work. Would that be true?

Albert Ellis: Yes. You could say that, in my life my work comes first, I come second, because I give up other pleasures for my work, and the woman in my life comes third. But Janet Wolfe is a beautiful and exceptionally important part of my life, which would be greatly bereft of laughter, warmth and intimacy without her.

Personal Characteristics

Windy Dryden: Let's move on to your personal characteristics. What are the main aspects of your personality?

Albert Ellis: I have always had a strong tendency to be vitally absorbed in something big ever since I can remember and get bored very easily when I'm not. I was vitally absorbed in light opera and musical comedy at 16 and in political activities at the age of 20. Then I got absorbed in the field of sex, love and marriage, and have written twenty books on the subject. I'm now absorbed in RET and am very involved in promulgating it as broadly as possible, since I think that it is probably the most effective form of therapy ever invented. This tendency to get involved also applies to my love relationships. But I've also got another major side too, as has been noted by Daniel Wiener, who called me a 'passionate sceptic'. So the other side of me that is very important is that I've always been exceptionally sceptical and non-devout. I'm even sceptical of RET. I'm sceptical of everything.

Windy Dryden: Has scepticism come naturally to you?

Albert Ellis: I think so. I used to believe in the Bible but gave that up at the age of 12, when I took a course in physical geography and found out that the world was millions of years old and that, consequently, the Bible was full of ——. I immediately became an atheist, and since that time I've been an involved atheist but not, I hope, a devout one.

Windy Dryden: You're often seen as abrasive and flamboyant, particularly in your lectures and public appearances. Would you agree with this view?

Albert Ellis: Well, abrasiveness and flamboyance are different. Let's start with abrasiveness. In lectures and workshops I'm much more abrasive than most people are, because they don't have the guts to speak their minds fully and I do. So if anyone asks me about Wilhelm Reich, for example, I'd say 'He was psychotic all his life,' which he was, and that some of his writings have some nauseating —— in them. So I'll say these things about people without hesitation. I don't think I'm abrasive face-to-face. In fact, I'm often quite the opposite and get along with people because I don't tell them about some of the things I think about them because I don't think they could easily handle them. In that sense I'm quite tactful. As a therapist I'm very strong and firm and sometimes abrasive in the sense that I'll get after people very strongly when I think that there is no other way of getting to them. Even then I unconditionally accept them but am just abrasive against their ideas. However, I usually get after people in a more gentle fashion. It depends on whom I'm working with. I take being flamboyant as meaning being unrestrained in a sort of dramatic, evocative manner, in which case I'm definitely flamboyant in that I often say things in humorous and startling ways.

Windy Dryden: Why do you do that?

Albert Ellis: Well, part of it is again that I'm courageous and will say publicly what others believe privately. But part of it is to stir up people, especially against Freudianism. I think the way to stir people up is to say something startling, in a dramatic way. I may antagonise some people by doing this, but I'm willing to take that risk.

Windy Dryden: Now in my own dealings with you, you seem to be rather gruff in your manner when we first meet but then you seem to slowly warm up to me. I'm not alone in having this impression. Is gruffness a side of your character that you recognise?

Albert Ellis: That's probably true to some degree, but a large part of it again comes back to the efficient use of time. When I see you or other people, you have questions for me, for example, and therefore I answer these quickly and efficiently and thus I may come across as gruff.

Windy Dryden: And yet in our written correspondence you are warmer and friendlier than you are in person.

Albert Ellis: That is probably because I have taken the time to do the letter and am not preoccupied with other things. When I spend time with Janet, for example, I have the time to be affectionate, warm or lightly humorous.

Windy Dryden: So the effective and efficient use of time really is extremely important to you?

Albert Ellis: That is correct.

Windy Dryden: Is there a vulnerable side to your character? For example, do you ever get discouraged or disillusioned?

Albert Ellis: I get disillusioned because I have illusions about people, which get clipped. For example, people sometimes act badly when at first they had acted quite well. So I get disillusioned, but I rarely get discouraged because I say 'Oh ——, that's not the way I saw it initially. Too damned bad.' And then I change some of the ideas I have about the person.

Windy Dryden: Would you describe yourself as sociable?

Albert Ellis: Well, I have more acquaintances than the great majority of people. Some who I see fairly regularly, like Ray DiGiuseppe and Dom DiMattia, are mainly involved in my work and professional life. Others who I'm not involved with professionally get short shrift because, again, I'm so involved with my own professional life. I get along with people but easily get bored with social conversation, which often tends to degenerate into idle chitchat. Besides Janet, I have very few real close friends, but that is mainly for lack of time.

Windy Dryden: Do you think you've missed out as a result of not having many close friends?

Albert Ellis: To some degree, but not seriously, because I get along very well without close friends and don't need to confide in people. I've never been that much of a confider.

Windy Dryden: You've often written about the value of having 'high frustration tolerance', the capacity to tolerate frustration in the service of working toward personal goals. How do you rate yourself on this characteristic?

Albert Ellis: Quite well. For example, I have diabetes. From the very first day I got it, I accepted it and did whatever I had to do to cope with it, namely, to take insulin and stick rigorously to a prescribed diet, which meant giving up quite a lot of foods that I liked. Consequently, after 35 years of having diabetes, I have practically no sequelae of it, and every diabetologist that I've seen thinks that I've done very well in keeping it under control.

Windy Dryden: Are there any areas where you have low frustration tolerance?

Albert Ellis: Yes. From time to time I still make myself angry at people when they act badly. I used to do this fairly frequently in the past, and it's rarer now, but I still do it. But I keep working at it and get over it very quickly when I do make myself angry, although I can still slip back into it.

Windy Dryden: That's interesting, because anger didn't arise in our discussion of your childhood – anxiety, worry and shyness did, but not anger. How do you account for that?

Albert Ellis: I don't remember being angry as a child and it may be that I squelched my anger because I was too anxious to let it out. I was certainly angry when I became a revolutionist in my teens, but it probably didn't bother me at the time. However, I was bothered about my anxiety.

Personal Reflections of a Professional Career

Windy Dryden: What [How] do you feel about what you've contributed to the field of psychotherapy?

Albert Ellis: I feel very happy that I have been the one who has been most instrumental in getting RET and cognitive behaviour therapy generally accepted, despite years of neglect and concerted opposition from practically everyone. I feel less happy that certain people have not given me credit; people like Wayne Dyer, whose best-selling book, *Your Erroneous Zones*, does not even mention RET but has taken about 98% from it. I also don't feel happy when the current cognitive–behaviour therapy literature mentions Aaron Beck or Donald Meichenbaum but doesn't mention me, and when Donald Meichenbaum, who used to cite me, will practically never cite me now. However, whether I'm given credit or not, my impact is still there, and I'm very pleased about that. It's too bad – but hardly awful – when I am neglected.

Windy Dryden: How would you like to be remembered after your death, when people reflect on the work of Albert Ellis?

Albert Ellis: In the field of psychotherapy, I would like them to say that I was the main pioneering cognitive and cognitive–behavioural theorist and therapist, that I fought very hard to get cognition accepted in psychotherapy, and that, largely as a result of my efforts, it has finally been accepted, albeit a little belatedly! Since I began, there has been a great deal of good research work in the field that might have come fifty years later without my pioneering efforts. Also, I'd like them to say that my work, directly with clients and indirectly through my writing, has helped an immense number of people. I'm very happy about that. My great contribution to the field of sex was that I was one of the real pioneers, along with Kinsey and others, in bringing about the sexual liberation revolution in the United States.

Windy Dryden: People tend to criticise you for being extremely repetitive in your writings. I've heard people say that you've repeated your ideas ad nauseam. Do you have any comments on that criticism?

Albert Ellis: I'm sure that is largely true not just of me but of others as well. The reason that I am so repetitive is that I accept invitations to write all kinds of articles on different aspects of RET in order to get RET ever more increasingly known.

Windy Dryden: You've alluded to your tendency to get bored easily. Don't you get rather bored by all that repetition?

Albert Ellis: Well, I may get bored to some degree, but I express myself differently each time so I minimise the boredom. But even if I did get bored, I would accept this boredom because I have a goal in repeating myself – which is to proselytise, to get the principles of RET over to an ever-wider audience.

Windy Dryden: Looking back over your professional career, are there things that you wished you'd done differently given hindsight?

Albert Ellis: Yes, probably. I'm not sure how it would have worked out, but if I'd been more political and had not been so honest about my opinion of certain people, including certain outstanding therapists and about other schools of therapy, that would have helped more. Carl Rogers, for example, was more circumspect in this regard. Whenever he was asked publicly about me or other therapists, he made no comment even though he must have had some pronounced views. By being so outspoken, I've helped get many people of opposing therapeutic schools very angry at me and consequently they've made up things about me – such as that I sleep with my female clients and that I have had eight wives. Quite false!

Windy Dryden: Will that mean that in the future you're going to be more tactful or do you think that the damage has been irreversibly done?

Albert Ellis: I think the damage has been done, and it would not do much good to change direction at this point, although I may be wrong about this.

Windy Dryden: Finally, the impression that you give to people through your productivity and your voracious appetite for work is that you are some kind of 'superman'. You've been able to produce many books, see many clients, and develop your other interests. When other working professionals look at what you've achieved, they do so with awe. Do you have any words of comfort for these less productive individuals?

Albert Ellis: Well, the reason why I've done so much and still, at the age of 75, get so much done is, I would say, largely the result of biology. First, I was born to two highly energetic parents who both lived reasonably long lives and were active until the last days of their lives. So I have a very high energy level, which has made it easier for me to do many more things than others. Second, I have another tendency, which we've discussed, to get vitally absorbed in what I'm interested in and this, coupled with my high energy, means that it's not hard to do as many things as I do. Other people may have neither a vital absorption in something nor high energy. Third, in many ways I have a very high frustration tolerance, as we've already discussed. When I write a book, for example, most of it is relatively easy and enjoyable for me to do, but when I come to making up the bibliography, I don't enjoy it as much as it is a pain in the ass to complete. But I just say '―― it', and I sit down and do it. My high frustration tolerance allows me to push through with projects, parts of which I really don't enjoy.

Windy Dryden: So your message to these less productive individuals is that you've been blessed with three strong biological tendencies that others may not have.

Albert Ellis: That's right. But don't forget my rational–emotive philosophy of life – which I have also worked hard to construct and to maintain.

References

ELLIS, A. (1986). Bibliography. *American Psychologist* 41, 380–397.

HEESACKER, M., HEPPNER, P.P. and ROGERS, M.E. (1982). Classics and emerging classics in counseling psychology. *Journal of Counseling Psychology* 29, 400–405.

SMITH, D. (1982). Trends in counseling and psychotherapy. *American Psychologist* 37, 802–809.

WEINRACH, S.G. (1980). Unconventional therapist. Albert Ellis. *Personnel and Guidance Journal* 59, 152–160.

Chapter 2
Who Am I to Teach Morals?
An Interview with Peter Lomas

Peter Lomas is married, has three children, and lives and works in Cambridge. He trained in medicine at Manchester, became senior neurosurgical house surgeon at the Manchester Royal Infirmary, and was a general practitioner for 6 years. He then trained at the Institute of Psychoanalysis, London. He has worked in a mental hospital, a child guidance clinic, a school for maladjusted adolescent boys and the Cassel Hospital, Richmond, where he studied post-partum breakdown and published a series of papers on the subject. This led to an interest in family therapy and in 1967 he edited *The Predicament of the Family* (Hogarth).

For the last 30 years Peter's main work has been as a psychotherapist in private practice. He is particularly interested in the nature of the psychotherapeutic relationship and has published three books on this subject: *True and False Experience* (Allen Lane, 1973); *The Case for a Personal Psychotherapy* (Oxford University Press, 1981) and *The Limits of Interpretation* (Penguin, 1987). His criticisms of the current technical approach towards emotional problems have led him to seek an alternative to the traditional training institutions. At present he is involved in a teaching set-up in which students are encouraged to use their own initiative in finding the optimal means by which they can learn psychotherapy.

Peter's aim is to understand the factors which stand in the way of an open and equal relationship between therapist and client and most of his writings focus on this question. He believes that professionals take for granted an unjustifiable superiority in conceiving what takes place between the two participants and explores some of these issues in the following interview.

Windy Dryden: OK, Peter, would you like to put the dilemma that you wish to talk to me about today in your own words?

Peter Lomas: Well, as I think about it at this moment, it is a very general dilemma concerning the question of where morality comes into psychotherapy. I am thinking particularly of the issue of how far one's own set of values actually influences what one is doing as a therapist. This matter is generally neglected in the literature. It seems to me that a therapist must have an aim for how he wants his patient to turn out to be. Although this question could quite easily be disposed of by saying that one wants the patient to be healthy instead of sick, this answer begs the question because one doesn't know what is the definition of health. Different people have different ideas about what constitutes health.

Windy Dryden: So you are saying then that the therapist's aims for the patient are more concrete than the vague notions of health.

Peter Lomas: Yes, I am. One can think in terms of health and sickness if there are fairly clear-cut aims that one might have in a therapeutic situation. If a patient comes along and says that he lies awake all night, then one would perhaps have the simple aim of helping him to sleep. However, in my experience with the people who come to me things are rarely as simple as that.

Windy Dryden: Presumably, the aims that you are talking about are influenced by the values of the therapist?

Peter Lomas: I think they are. I work in long-term therapy so I am not trying to achieve a quick cure of simple problems, because the people who come to me are usually those whose lives have gone badly astray, who have become lost and want to find their way in life. I have some idea in my mind of the kind of people I want them to turn out to be. I don't mean in detail, I don't mean that I may want someone to become prime minister or anything like that! However, I think I have consciously or unconsciously the aim that I would want him to become the kind of person that I admire, the kind of person that I like, the kind of person that I might want to be with. I think that means that he or she would (if I can influence him or her) end up as having values about living which are rather similar to my own. To put it in general terms (which might seem rather pompous) I suppose I would like him or her to end up as a 'good' person in a moral sense, good according to standards that I, and perhaps many other people, would find acceptable, that many philosophers and religious teachers might regard as virtuous. Someone, for example, who believes in truth, who doesn't lie.

Windy Dryden: Now, in what way is this a dilemma for you? You are saying that your aim is fairly clear, you do have in mind what kind of person you would like your patient to be, and this is in part determined by your own values. Now, where in this topic is the dilemma for you?

Peter Lomas: Well, I think in two ways. First, because I don't set myself up publicly as a sort of preacher, a dispenser of morals, like a clergyman would who has a set of Christian morals. People don't come to me for that kind of thing. I feel a little as if I am a kind of priest in disguise – a priest in the very broadest of terms, not a Christian priest. It could be said that I am in the business of 'character building'. I don't subject my patients to cold showers or cross-country runs but I'm just as concerned to build their characters as the traditional boarding-school headmaster.

Second, which is perhaps just a different way of putting it, I don't know that I have a right to impose my moral system of beliefs on somebody else. I wouldn't particularly like someone else to come and do that to me. I don't mind talking to people about morals and listening to people whom I respect talk about how to live, but I would not want to put myself in a vulnerable position where I might be influenced to adopt a set of beliefs that belong to them.

Windy Dryden: So, on the one hand you are saying that you would like your patients to turn out to be 'good' in the moral sense and yet on the other hand you don't want to be in a situation where you are imposing this value system on them?

Peter Lomas: Yes, that's right. That is where I feel the dilemma to be. I know I want to influence the person and I know I am going to try to do it. I can't help trying to do it. People come to therapy to be influenced in some kind of way and I can't just shut up and do nothing and leave them as they are. I suppose in certain areas it is not such a problem because if it is very broad then many people would perhaps agree with my view of things and the patient himself might actually hope to be changed in certain ways. Let us say that the person steals, then I don't, if it's a straightforward case, feel particularly uneasy about trying to influence him by whatever means, some of it by self-understanding, some of it by helping him to feel more secure so that he doesn't need to steal. I wouldn't feel much discomfort at having to argue my case for changing him into a person who no longer steals because I would imagine that most people would say that that is a good change; and he himself, particularly if he didn't find himself in court so often, might see it as a change for the better. However, I think there are many other situations which are not so clear-cut.

One such issue concerns the question of conformity versus rebellion, where there exist no laws, unless rebellion goes to an extent that laws are broken, and people and property are damaged. I think that by nature I am a bit of a rebel, a bit of a non-conformist in some ways. People who come to see me sometimes talk about the question of whether they should revolt against a certain situation. I am thinking of a man I saw yesterday who had some dealings with a hospital as a patient. He questioned the doctor about his treatment, but was worried about making a nuisance of himself. He wondered whether he had a right to challenge the authorities or whether he should go along with what was being done. This seems to fall within the general framework of morals. It is concerned with how one should live, like the issue of the banning of trade unions at GCHQ at Cheltenham. One could imagine having a discussion about such issues and asking: 'What is the right moral attitude here? Should one conform as far as possible to the laws of the land and make life harmonious or should one challenge them and try to change them?'

Windy Dryden: Are you saying then that in the particular instance with your patient who is faced with a choice of whether or not to challenge the hospital system that, because you tend to have values that favour challenge and rebellion, this might influence the way you discuss the topic with him, perhaps in the direction of encouraging him, albeit subtly, to take a challenging stance rather than a conformity stance?

Peter Lomas: Yes, I think that does happen and if it doesn't happen openly it happens, as you say, subtly. If I don't speak openly about my views, the patient will no doubt discern them by my responses, perhaps my non-verbal responses, my tone of voice, bits of approval and so on. I think my values will become evident. Whether I choose to make interpretations or not will be revealing. On the whole, like other analytically oriented therapists, I interpret things if I think that the patient's behaviour is abnormal or inappropriate in some fashion. Thus, for instance, if I thought that this man was challenging the doctor inappropriately, then I wouldn't come out with my own opinions directly, but I might make an interpretation. I might say: 'Well, isn't it an example of how you never came to terms with your father's authority, and you are still fighting him?' Whereas if I thought his behaviour was appropriate, I don't think I would make that interpretation or any other.

Windy Dryden: So, what you seem to be saying then, is that the response that therapists make, like interpretations, are very much guided by their own explicit, or implicit, value systems. If that is so, since your values do affect your behaviour and since you do have in mind what you are trying to do with your patients, to what extent then do you publicly say: 'Look, this is the kind of person I am, these are the kind of beliefs and values that I have. These are the kind of beliefs and values that I think I would like my patients to have'?

Peter Lomas: I think that is a very relevant question, because one thing I believe very passionately about psychotherapy is that whatever the therapist does she must try not to confuse the patient. It seems to me that many people who come for therapy are confused; perhaps all of them are confused to some extent. They are not sure of their own perceptions. There are theories derived from work with families about how people have come to doubt their own perceptions because they have been placed in double-bind positions. I think that one of the ways in which a therapist can help a patient is to enable her to sort out these confusions. In order to do that I think she must make sure that she doesn't confuse the patient by, for instance, saying one thing and doing another. Or by pretending she doesn't have views – that she is quite neutral – when she really does. If that happens the patient will pick up cues which indicate that the therapist is incongruent and will become even more confused, especially if he is fearful of challenging the therapist.

Windy Dryden: So, you would not encourage the therapist to adopt a line of neutrality, because that would be confusing for the patient because underneath this neutrality the therapist does have a set of values, and somehow by not making these explicit the patient will become confused – a situation that will presumably have a deleterious effect on his or her mental health. OK then, to what extent are you going openly to disclose your values?

Peter Lomas: Well here we come to one of the dilemmas, because to take it to an extreme, I would think it quite wrong for me to get up on a soapbox and start lecturing the patient about how people should live, telling him or her all about my beliefs. That would seem quite inappropriate because it would be imposing my values on them, and doing so when they are in a vulnerable state.

Windy Dryden: That's the 'imposing' model that you were talking about earlier and that's what you don't want to do?

Peter Lomas: I don't want to do it, so somehow, it seems to me, I have to find a way in which I am not shouting my views at patients or trying to indoctrinate them, but a way in which I am also not hiding my views to such an extent that I become confusing to them. I think many of the problems that one comes up against in therapy are rather similar to the kind of problems one comes up against as a parent with children. One has to find a middle way in which one doesn't try to brainwash people into accepting one's views, but also one would not try, as parents tend to do, to conceal things.

Windy Dryden: So, on the one hand, we have this 'confusion' model whereby the therapist has values, and yet in adopting a neutral stance pretends that she doesn't have them. On the other hand, there is the 'imposing' model, the 'soapbox' model, where you stand up and lecture the patient about how he or she should live. Now, what you seem to advocate is some sort of middle ground. However, I am not clear about the nature of that middle ground, I'm finding it elusive at the moment. I wonder if you could elucidate it?

Peter Lomas: I will try. I sympathise with your finding it elusive because I think it *is* elusive. It is something that one has to struggle with. I think it has a lot to do with establishing a kind of open dialogue with the person, in which as far as possible there is an equality. If a therapist is open he can discuss what is happening between him and the patient; how they are coming to the conclusions that they come to; why the patient might believe something; why the therapist, on the other hand, might disagree. If one is going to give the patient the optimum conditions for trusting his own perceptions then it is incumbent upon the therapist to be open. In other words, I think he should not only be open if challenged about how he feels people should live, but also admit his doubts about it, and explain to the best of his ability why he holds certain views. Then the two people could have a discussion about it.

Windy Dryden: Would this also include the notion that there were other ways of living one's life? For example, I can imagine with the patient that you referred to earlier you might say something like this: 'Well, look, in this situation because I value standing up and making a fuss I guess I might have done that. However, there are other ways. There is the way of X and there is the way of Y. Now I guess your goal is actually to find the course of action that fits in with your values, but I don't want to hide from you the fact that I value this course of action and yet I don't want to impose my views upon you.'

Peter Lomas: That's right. Yes I like the way you put that. It gives the patient a chance to make his own estimation of another person who he might respect and who is being open with him. However, he also needs to know in what ways the therapist might be prejudiced. He needs to be able to make his own critique of the therapist's position which would then perhaps help him to establish where he stands. As a result of this kind of approach (as you can perhaps guess) I do find myself having quite long and detailed discussions in therapy about such things as the morality of abortion. If a patient is thinking of having an abortion, the more traditional psychoanalytic approach would be not to discuss the merits and demerits of abortion but to interpret this in the context of the patient's personal history: to look for whatever in their own lives might have led them to fear bringing up a baby, with the result that they perhaps unconsciously are having the abortion not for the reasons they are giving but because there is some deeper reason that makes them fear holding a baby in their arms – or something like that. That seems to me the sort of interpretive method which I would criticise.

Windy Dryden: Which is based on the notion that the normative value is that the woman is naturally drawn to bringing up children?

Peter Lomas: That's right. I certainly wouldn't question an exploration of all the things that have gone into making the patient feel one way or another. But I feel there is an awful danger with that approach (as I think you are saying to me) of accepting a norm which the patient may need to be able to question.

Windy Dryden: Let's say as a result of this open discussion of values the patient chooses a way that for example is opposite to yours. So if you value rebelliousness he or she might choose the conforming way; if you value truth he or she might choose the deceptive way. Is that a dilemma for you?

Peter Lomas: Yes.

Windy Dryden: In what way?

Peter Lomas: It is a dilemma because I don't know how far I should let the patient go his own way – a way which I don't approve of. I don't know how far I should try to stop him. In a way it is the question of how much one stands back, feeling that the person's freedom is very important even if he is going to do something that appears to you self-destructive.

Windy Dryden: Which is a value in itself?

Peter Lomas: Yes. A freedom to live one's own life however one does it. It is a value. So I am torn between letting that happen and saying nothing or pointing out ways in which I think they might be misguided, ways which might lead them into trouble. These are very similar dilemmas to those one has in ordinary life with one's family and friends; it is just that I think in psychotherapy they tend to be obscured by theory. In day-to-day psychotherapy such matters as whether one should marry somebody or not are being discussed as they would with one's family and friends.

Windy Dryden: I wonder if one of the theories which tends to obscure this problem in psychotherapy is the theory that states that the preferred role of the therapist should be that of a facilitator. This theory states that the goal of the therapist is not to impose or even necessarily bring out one's own value systems but to help the client find their own way no matter what way that might turn out to be. Perhaps most of the time the client may find a way which society in general would call 'good' and moral but at times the client would go off in a self-destructive way and if that happens so be it. It is not necessarily the therapist's task to say: 'Hey wait a minute but that's the wrong way.' Is that one of the theories that might obscure this issue, would you say?

Peter Lomas: I think it does. I think it obscures the issue because it implies that one can be a neutral facilitator. First, I don't believe one can be neutral and, second, I believe even if one takes a neutral stand it could at times be immoral to sit back and let someone do something very destructive. The ultimate example would be suicide. If one really thought a patient would commit suicide and was going to do so for stupid reasons, sick reasons, it would seem to me that I would want to do something or say something to stop him. I might even take drastic action.

Windy Dryden: What implications does what you are talking about have on the way therapists actually establish a therapeutic enterprise with their patients?

Peter Lomas: I think quite a lot, because the way the therapist behaves and the expectations she has of the patient show to quite a degree, I think, her moral stance in life, and in society. Whether for instance she believes that people are equal; whether she believes in hierarchies; what her attitude is to professionalism; what her attitude is to intimacy; to what extent she feels people should be open and close with each other, or not; what she believes about money. The way she dresses is as revealing as is the way she speaks to the client. Does she, for example, believe in gentleness or roughness? Is she a permissive kind of person who is going to give a lot of space to the patient, or is she someone who will go in for a lot of confrontation and challenge? These issues might have something to do with her theoretical beliefs and technique, it might be something to do with her personality – the way she is made – but it also seems to be something to do with the moral stance she takes about how people should behave with each other.

Windy Dryden: If you set up a psychotherapeutic enterprise, where you are going to make explicit these things, you may very well lose a number of clients, who, for example, don't think it is your job actually to disclose your beliefs, or want you to act in a different way, or don't value at the beginning the kind of things that you value. Therefore you cannot establish a therapeutic alliance with them.

Peter Lomas: Well, I find that rather rare. I find that when people come to me they don't usually break off, and I suspect that part of that has to do with selection.

Windy Dryden: I was just going to mention that. Your referral network might be helpful in this respect in that they might say: 'We'll send this person to Peter, he or she is the sort of person who we think is going to get on with Peter, is going to share some of his beliefs.'

Peter Lomas: I think that is true. This wouldn't happen if I was working in the Health Service; I have worked for the Health Service in the past so I've some experience of that kind. It would be less likely to happen if I were working in London rather than in a relatively small city where people can get to know me and my beliefs. And it is likely to happen because I write. Quite a number of my clients come to me because they have either read what I have written or because they have been recommended to me by a friend. So I think there is a certain amount of selection in that. It would be rather nice for me to believe that I was such a great therapist that people don't break off. That could have its hazards couldn't it? It could be that I collude in some way to keep them, but yes, I think selection plays a big part in what you mention.

Windy Dryden: So therapists who work more anonymously had better face the fact that if they are going openly to disclose values, and conduct therapy according to these values, they may not be able to establish a therapeutic alliance with clients who at the very outset are going to share a different morality, a different value system so that coming together may not be viable?

Peter Lomas: It may be a problem. I haven't thought of it as much of a problem because it is not as though a therapist working as I do gets particularly known for, say, his political beliefs. If I were a very strong Marxist, for instance, then that could lead me into trouble, but even if I were I don't think I would announce it.

Windy Dryden: However, if you were a Marxist and a client was talking about adding yet another factory to his empire that might cause you a dilemma.

Peter Lomas: Yes, I think it would, and I think I would have to be tactful. That might sound a rather unscientific, messy and uncourageous way of doing it, but I think that particularly at the early stages with clients if one confronted them very quickly with diametrically opposed views then one might lose them or it might be so upsetting that they would shut up; and that wouldn't be therapeutic. However, the sooner I could get to telling them where I stood the better.

Windy Dryden: So let me see if I can sum up what you seem to be talking about today. As a therapist you neither want to impose values on your clients, nor do you want to remain neutral. You want actually to let patients know where you stand on things, you want to show that there are alternatives, and that when they take those alternatives that is a dilemma for you because it confronts you with the notion that patients may proceed in ways that you from your value system deem to be self-destructive, and in this circumstance you may very well try to stop them doing this. Does that seem to be the way that you have actually solved this dilemma for yourself?

Peter Lomas: Yes, there are certainly instances where I would not disclose.

Windy Dryden: What might some of these instances be?

Peter Lomas: Well I suppose they would be instances in which I would feel perhaps insecure in my own view and so I would let the thing go for better or for worse. It also occurs to me that I would hold back my own view sometimes if I thought it was going to be particularly painful, traumatically painful, to another person. If somebody had done something which I thought was a heinous crime I might play that down because I wouldn't want at that moment to increase the guilt he already feels. I would hope later on, when he was in better shape, that we would discuss it more openly and both admit that what had been done was terrible.

Windy Dryden: I guess from what you were saying earlier, there is always a risk in so doing that the patient is going to be confused, because on the one hand you are not giving a view and on the other they may sense that view.

Peter Lomas: Yes I would feel very uneasy doing that and I do it to the very minimum. I'm only saying that sometimes I do do it.

Windy Dryden: So there are pragmatic grounds which may intervene and stop you from saying: 'Well, this is my moral principle.'

Peter Lomas: That's right. If there's one thing that guides me in this it's the thought that I must use common sense in therapy just as much as in ordinary living.

Chapter 3
The Two-plus-one Model
An Interview with Michael Barkham

Michael Barkham initially trained as a teacher, obtaining his first degree in education at Sussex (BEd) before completing a degree in experimental psychology at Cambridge (MA). He carried out his doctoral research in counselling psychology on the topic of perceived empathy at Brighton Polytechnic (PhD). This work, which was an early example of the events paradigm, investigated critical moments in counselling and was predicated on the assumption that our understanding of the subtleties of the counselling process could be advanced by adopting rigorous research techniques.

On completing his doctoral programme, he was awarded a regional scholarship to carry out training in clinical psychology at Surrey University (MSc), before taking up post as a research clinical psychologist to work in the psychotherapy team led by Professor David Shapiro at the MRC/ESRC Social and Applied Psychology Unit at the University of Sheffield. A major part of his time has been involved in carrying out the Second Sheffield Psychotherapy Project, a major process of outcome investigation contrasting two orientations of therapy (cognitive–behavioural and relationship-oriented) and two durations (eight and sixteen sessions). His interest in cost-effective interventions has been extended to the development of a form of very brief therapy termed the two-plus-one model in which clients are seen for two sessions one week apart followed by a third session three months later. He is currently engaged in a major process–outcome study of the two-plus-one model. In addition to carrying out these studies, he has steered concurrent replications of both these studies with colleagues in the NHS.

In 1991 he was promoted to a career appointment with the Medical Research Council. He has written, as sole author or in collaboration, approximately 30 scientific papers, book chapters and articles spanning the disciplines of clinical psychology, counselling psychology and psychotherapy. He was the 1992 recipient of the May Davidson Award from the British Psychological Society Division of Clinical Psychology for his contributions to the field of psychotherapy. He is currently UK Vice-President Elect of the Society for Psychotherapy Research and is currently on the Board of Examiners for the British Psychological Society's Diploma in Counselling Psychology. Although his research interests extend widely in the areas of psychotherapy, including aspects of clients' interpersonal problems and the assimilation of clients' problematic experiences, his current work in developing and investigating both the potential and the limitations of the two-plus-one model represents one of his major current research and clinical occupations.

Windy Dryden: Can we start the interview by my asking you to describe the nature of the two-plus-one model that was developed in Sheffield?

Michael Barkham: The model we have developed at SAPU [Social and Applied Psychology Unit] arose from our wish to address two issues: one academic and one practitioner-oriented. Perhaps it is more useful to focus on the latter because that has more direct relevance to practitioners in the field. What we were concerned about was how to deliver a high-impact but low-cost treatment to clients. We looked at the research literature to try and identify the most effective components in devising a model of therapy. On various criteria derived from the literature, we developed the two-plus-one model which comprises two sessions of therapy one week apart followed by a third session three months later. The rationale for the model stems from our knowing that there is a high impact on clients early in therapy and that subsequently there are diminishing returns. The longer one sees a client, effectively, the less improvement one is getting; one is getting into 'fine tuning' and what we wanted was a high-impact treatment in order to reach as many people as possible as quickly as possible in order to reduce waiting lists. In other words, to devise a delivery system in which people who wanted treatment could be seen as quickly as possible via an effective treatment model which would either act as a 'holding environment' until more long-term treatment became available, or was sufficient as a 'treatment episode' in itself to address their immediate problems.

Windy Dryden: To what extent was the impetus for the development of the model the desire to reduce waiting lists?

Michael Barkham: In terms of offering a model to practitioners it was a primary concern. The point is that there is an ethical issue with waiting lists: if treatment is to be offered, one usually views it as being offered to individuals. Actually, it should be available to people in the community, and I think that, however effective treatments are on a one-to-one basis, we have to weigh that against how many people out in the community are not being seen at the same time as one person is being seen by a single counsellor.

Windy Dryden: So would it be correct to say that the model was developed mainly for clinical psychologists in the health service where waiting lists are particularly problematic?

Michael Barkham: Certainly that was the context we had in mind and so that was clearly our primary practical concern although there were more 'academic' considerations.

Windy Dryden: Later, we'll consider the range of convenience of the model. Perhaps we can look at the question of the structure of the model. First, why is it two-plus-one and not, for example, three-plus-two? Second, why is the interim period one of three months rather than three and one-half or two and one-half months? I'm interested to hear about the fine tuning of the model and the reasons for its precise form.

Michael Barkham: In a sense, one could provide a rationale for other models, but the point is that they need to be evaluated and tested in the field and that is what we are currently aiming to do with the two-plus-one model. So what I am saying is that it is not sufficient to come up with the rationale alone; one then has to evaluate the model and that is what we are currently doing. But in terms of the rationale for the two-plus-one model, we were not interested in devising the briefest possible therapy, for example, a single-session intervention. What we wanted to do was to capture the process of therapy, and our view was that if you tried to have a 'one-shot' intervention, then, yes, you would get a lot of information about the session but you wouldn't get information on the progression from one session to another, of elapsed time itself. So we were not interested in going for a one-session set-up as, for example, Alvin Mahrer does.

Windy Dryden: Even though the literature might indicate that it might be possible?

Michael Barkham: Yes. I'm sure one could develop a rationale for saying that actually a one-hour, two-hour or three-hour session would be useful but it would accumulate or summate a different kind of information about the psychotherapeutic process than that which we were primarily interested in.

Windy Dryden: Right, so you were not only interested in offering a brief model of therapy, but also a model which would in some way tap into the process of psychotherapy?

Michael Barkham: Yes, all along there was a research rationale in which we were not only trying to offer effective treatment to people, but also wanting to devise a cost-effective research model. Doing psychotherapy research is very expensive and we wanted to offer an effective service in tandem with providing a summary of the psychotherapeutic process for research purposes which actually captured the core components of the psychotherapeutic process. We wanted to be able to evaluate the whole model without having to select bits and pieces of the process. That was of great interest to us. There are a number of strands there which all pulled into our devising that particular model.

So, having excluded a single session model of therapy, we looked at the literature on the dose–effect curve in psychotherapy which shows the diminishing returns the longer clients remain in therapy. After two sessions the data indicate that 30 per cent of clients show 'measurable improvement', with three sessions likely to produce a figure of approximately 36 per cent; in other words, about one in three clients. After that, the additional percentage of clients who show improvement reduces after each successive session although obviously the total increases. So, it seemed to us that at the very minimal level of two and three sessions, there was a strong rationale to suggest that this was an effective number of sessions to offer. Now it also seemed to us that it was not just about offering a specific number of sessions because there is literature suggesting that change occurs as a function of elapsed time and it seemed to us that rather than just offering two or three sessions consecutively each week, we could incorporate the notion of elapsed time into the model so that we could provide a model which had a high impact at the beginning with the two sessions and which then provided the clients with a framework, a structure, to go away and work by themselves knowing that they were going to come back for a third session three months later. So this was the rationale and it seemed to us to be substantially different from offering just two sessions alone.

Now, your next question is going to be 'Why three months?'. In a way, that is as much a clinical hunch as anything. We discussed this with Bob Hobson when we were developing the model and three months seemed to be a period of time which was sufficiently long for clients to have to work on their own. There is a temptation to offer less; in other words, one asks oneself 'Is it all right to let this client go three months?'. One might be tempted, clinically, to see the client in four or six weeks. Our hunch was that there would be many clients who would, understandably, 'hang on' for that third session without doing any work, and our intention was to try and utilise the clients' capacity to work on their own in order to reduce the dependency on the therapy or the therapist. With a period of three months we felt they would have to work on their own. Now this refers back to what I was saying earlier about evaluation; this component needs to be researched. If we had infinite resources, we would want to test out a two-month gap a one-month gap and so on.

Windy Dryden: So, just to recap, the model was initially developed mainly for use in clinical psychology departments in the NHS and mainly to reduce the phenomenon of waiting lists. The structure of the two-plus-one model, with two sessions one week apart and the third session three months later, can be justified on the basis of the research literature; although it is also based upon clinical hunches. However, you also recognise that equally one could make a case from the research literature for the development of a four-plus-two model with a two-month gap. Therefore, you are not saying that the two-plus-one model is the best model that the research literature advocates.

Michael Barkham: No, there is nothing sacred in that way about the model.

Windy Dryden: You wanted to capture the process and you also wanted to give clients the opportunity to do some work on their own. Is that accurate?

Michael Barkham: Yes.

Windy Dryden: Now, moving away from the area of clinical psychology just for a moment, let us look at the model's potential for counselling psychologists. What would you say the model has to offer counselling psychologists?

Michael Barkham: Looking at the overall rationale for the model, it seems that much of it derives from the ethos within community psychology, that is, the rationale that existed in the States for providing a service to the community. It seems to me that this kind of model has currency where the discipline values people, independent of their psychological well-being. In other words, it is not just about the throughput of clients and trying to reduce waiting lists, but about how to present a service delivery system to the community at large – how to try and improve the psychological well-being of people within the community. In this way, one is developing a model of service akin to, for example, dentists or any other particular service where one is saying: 'Here is a facility, here is a service which is there for you to use to enhance your psychological well-being and that to use it you do not have to label yourself "psychiatrically disturbed" or "psychologically distressed".' Rather, it is a matter of saying 'Here is a resource; can I use this to enhance my current psychological state?' and to do so across the different stages of one's life span. This is where the model can be developed and incorporated into counselling psychology. However, I think there are some aspects of the model which some counselling psychologists may not feel totally comfortable with, but I think the model can be adapted and incorporated into the ethos of counselling psychology.

Windy Dryden: Let's have a closer look at that. You mentioned that there would be certain elements of the model that you predict counselling psychologists would be uncomfortable with. What do you think those aspects would be?

Michael Barkham: I think probably one of the main ones is, and this point is not specific to this model alone, the fact that one has a set model and one is providing a model almost irrespective of what the person's presenting needs are. I think there would be counselling psychologists who would say that you should devise an implicit model in response to each person's presenting problems.

Windy Dryden: So, in a sense the criticism might be that you are fitting the client to the model rather than the model to meet the client's needs.

Michael Barkham: Yes, good point.

Windy Dryden: How would you respond to that criticism?

Michael Barkham: I think ultimately I would say that it is an empirical question and needs to be tested. I can understand the argument, but I think, and this applies to counselling psychology in general, that we need more evaluation. I think there are assumptions that actually need to be tested and I think counselling psychology has to be sufficiently robust to be able to evaluate them and then, in the light of the outcome, adapt itself accordingly. For example, do clients actually object to the model? Is it a problem for clients? Do some clients find it useful? Who are those clients?

Windy Dryden: So, in effect, what you are saying is that you recognise that there may be objections on the grounds that you are fitting the client to the model, but your response is 'Well, I understand that, but let's look at the data; let's look at the evidence. Maybe the evidence won't suggest that. Indeed, perhaps the evidence may challenge a cherished idea that counselling psychologists have?'

Michael Barkham: Indeed, it's the same kind of logic as the investigations into the Rogerian 'necessary and sufficient' conditions, for example, that were sacred components of counselling psychology in the States and subsequent research findings were rather equivocal about their relationship to successful outcome.

Windy Dryden: Although I think the major difference there is that what was being researched was an idea that emerged from a philosophy about how to work and be with clients. That brings us to the philosophy that underlies the two-plus-one model, one which you recognise may be anathema to counselling psychologists.

Michael Barkham: Sure, but my argument basically is, let's evaluate and see and bring back evaluation into the discipline of counselling psychology.

Windy Dryden: You seem to be saying to counselling psychologists: 'Look, this model doesn't come out of the air, it does have some empirical justification, so in a sense if we want to be counselling psychologists, we really do need to be responsive to what the research literature has to offer. Let's evaluate the extent to which this model can be effective while leaving the idea of adapting any model to the client's needs to one side.'

Michael Barkham: Yes, that is my preference, because I think that counselling psychology needs to heighten its research component and to adopt a more evaluative (i.e. research rather than judgemental) frame of reference.

Windy Dryden: And this might be one way of doing that. Now I think this question really needs to be looked at as having relevance for both counselling psychologists and clinical psychologists. To what extent would you want to see this model being applied to all those who are seeking psychological help, or to what extent would you want there to be set criteria for clients who are going to be offered the two-plus-one intervention?

Michael Barkham: Well, in a way those are two separate strategies and one can adopt either of them depending on resources.

Windy Dryden: Well, let's look at them one at a time. Let's look at the 'two-plus-one for everybody' case. Are you saying that this would be a legitimate approach for a clinic or perhaps an individual to take?

Michael Barkham: Yes. If you're under-resourced and you have got a high demand, whether that's in the clinic or on an individual basis, if your aim is to reach as many of the people who are seeking help as quickly as possible (given the research evidence that the sooner people are seen, the better the outcome), then I think that there is a professional argument for saying 'I am going to offer the two-plus-one model to everybody. For some of those (maybe up to one-third according to the research literature), that would be sufficient; it would provide them with the basis for going away and working by themselves and making use of their existing social support networks. Other people will need more and that is fine; resources can then be allocated to them.' One then develops and moves on to further models for the delivery of counselling or therapy having used the initial two-plus-one model as an assessment of the person's ability to respond to this mode of counselling, or provide the basis for believing that they might respond better to another modality. In a way, it's not solely a treatment model; but rather in these latter instances it becomes a therapeutic assessment procedure.

Windy Dryden: OK. Let's remain with the case where one is offering the 'two-plus-one' model to everybody, recognising that if you adopt that strategy, approximately one-third of the people who you are going to see are going to be helped, but for two-thirds of them that may not be sufficient. Now, as you know, there is also a literature on client deterioration. When might clients not be offered the two-plus-one intervention? When to do so might lead to deterioration?

Michael Barkham: In terms of the particular model itself, we have deliberately excluded people who present with psychotic or obsessive–compulsive problems. Those are two primary contraindicators for offering the model and for whom we feel the model would not be appropriate.

Windy Dryden: What about acutely depressed and suicidal clients?

Michael Barkham: Well, that's an interesting case because, on the one hand, you might intuitively feel that it couldn't be useful, but, on the other, if you stick with the rationale that what can be most effective is to offer something quickly, you adopt the rationale of crisis intervention which is exactly how you might present the model to people in this instance. So in fact a powerful and immediate delivery to people who are presenting with those kinds of problems may well be a very significant contribution, particularly if one evaluates the intervention in terms of 'how likely are they now to attempt suicide?'. They may still be presenting with a high level of depression, but they may be at a significantly lower risk of committing suicide. In this case, one might evaluate the intervention as being successful.

Windy Dryden: What are the characteristics of this third of clients for whom the two-plus-one model might be sufficient?

Michael Barkham: Well, in a way the question is a bit in advance of our ability to answer because the study we are carrying out at SAPU to address this question is still underway. One of our aims is to be able to determine those clients for whom the model is likely to be most successful. So, to date, we don't have the empirical data to answer that question. The research literature suggests that there might be one-third of clients who would benefit from the model.

Windy Dryden: But it's not clear at the moment what characteristics this third may have.

Michael Barkham: Exactly. We could postulate that they are likely to be people who can utilise their own resources well, so we could say they have good ego strength or they are well resourced or they may have good social networks which they haven't actually been utilising. One can predict that they are likely to be people who are highly motivated, and who can build upon the initial two sessions. But these are hunches and we haven't analysed sufficient data yet.

Windy Dryden: Let's then look at the second scenario, and that is this. We are not going to offer this model to everybody; we are going to select clients. What inclusion or exclusion criteria do you suggest?

Michael Barkham: Well, in a way that relates to what we were just talking about trying to pull out from the study we are engaged in. So, in a way we are still in the area of clinical hunches and working from the cases we have seen already. Our experience is such that we have only delivered this model to people who score below a certain threshold on a particular screening measure. We have not, for example, offered it to people who are severely depressed.

Windy Dryden: Although you could.

Michael Barkham: Yes. I'm not saying we couldn't; it is simply that we have not progressed to that stage yet. We believe in testing aspects of the model's applicability in a stagewise process. However, in Bolton Clinical Psychology Department, they have been using this in a field setting with clients with a higher level of depression and they have been finding cases of success, but equally cases where it has not been sufficient in itself.

Windy Dryden: Let's suppose that I am a practising clinical or counselling psychologist and I like the idea of the model. Moreover, I want to experiment with using it but don't want to offer it to everybody. I come to you for guidance and ask you what inclusion and exclusion criteria I should use. What would you say to me?

Michael Barkham: OK, I think two points. The first is about overall evaluation. How severely distressed is this person? How severely depressed or anxious are they? There is a severity continuum which I think is important to bear in mind. So you have to have some information, whether it's on a screening measure or a statement from the client or whatever about the severity of his or her presenting problems. The second point about selection of clients for the model would be those people who are presenting with a quite focused problem and this relates to how one works in the two-plus-one model. In working with the model, one selects a focus and works primarily with that one focus. If a client is presenting with a multitude of problems which appear not to be well focused, they're very vague and the client is not sure in what area the problem is, then I would suspect that they do not have a good prospect for working with the model. However, if a client is presenting with a particularly focused issue – in some way they know what the area is although they may not know exactly what it is but are able to target it in some way – then one might have a relatively good outlook for those clients in the model.

Windy Dryden: Right, so the first criterion is the severity of the presenting problems and the second one is the ability to work with a major focus or certainly not too many foci. If clients have a myriad of different problems or if they talk about an overall vague sense of distress without being able to isolate or identify specific foci, these would not be very good candidates for the two-plus-one intervention.

Michael Barkham: Those two criteria may well be quite highly correlated in some way. But I think you could equally well try it with clients who are severely distressed but actually quite highly focused. These would be the 'borderline' cases.

Windy Dryden: Right, I'm still this notional clinical or counselling psychologist. I like the model. I am either going to implement an 'open door' policy or I am going to select out those clients whom we have just discussed. Where do I go from here? What do I need to do to prepare myself to put this model into practice?

Michael Barkham: Do you mean in terms of logistics or do you mean from when you are sitting down with a client?

Windy Dryden: Well both. Let's take the macro question first. What kind of system do I need to implement first before I can start investigating the usefulness or the effectiveness of the model?

Michael Barkham: I think in terms of the logistics of working in the model, one has to develop a rationale and some basic literature which may well be useful to clients. In other words, one needs to be able effectively to select out those clients for whom the model is not appropriate. Then I think if you decide that you want to offer this person two-plus-one therapy, then they need a written rationale saying exactly what it is that they are going to receive. The rationale can be quite short, but it has to be clear so that the client knows what is going to happen. This relates to the question of immediacy because the client, rather than being put on a waiting list, receives a notification that he or she is going to be offered two appointments with specific dates together with a rationale for this delivery and how it might help him or her. That in itself will have an impact on many clients; they are already receiving counselling or treatment because they are in a delivery system; something is going to happen for them and they know when it will happen. That is an important aspect. They will then respond to that either by saying 'Yes, I want to take up this offer' or not. I think one has to offer it to them; they have the right to decline it and that's where, if they do decline it, one has then to fall back on an alternative model.

Windy Dryden: Right, so as a therapist I will need to prepare myself by developing a rationale which I can send to clients explaining the model, its purpose, and what's going to happen so that I can ask for their informed consent.

Michael Barkham: Yes, they have to be able to respond and say 'Yes, I want to take up this offer of counselling'. Taking that a bit further, in the current study one of the conditions includes presenting clients, before therapy, with a manual about their specific role. In other words, offering clients a document to read through which tells them what is likely to happen for themselves as a client during the sessions. That is an interesting development because it is likely that this will increase the potentcy of the delivery system.

Windy Dryden: And is firmly rooted in the literature which shows that preparing clients for therapy is helpful in itself.

Michael Barkham: That is one of the clearest research findings and yet is very little used in clinical practice.

Windy Dryden: If I adopt the 'open door' policy, I can send this letter to anybody who is seeking help because I am not making any assessment concerning whether or not some clients are going to be suitable, so I don't need to assess a client because I have this open door policy; I am going to offer everyone the two-plus-one intervention, right?

Michael Barkham: Yes, but if you are going to do that I would advise you to collect information on clients' presenting problems or severity levels. I think if one is presenting an open door policy where the model is offered to everybody, I would want some self-report information on those clients – for example, a measure of general presenting problems.

Windy Dryden: You mean before I sent out the letter explaining the two-plus-one model?

Michael Barkham: No, in tandem with it. If it was the policy of the practitioner or the department that, irrespective of the presenting problems of clients, they were going to be offered the model, that would clearly be stated in the rationale. For example, 'It is the policy of this department initially to see people within this model because clients can be seen very quickly and we believe this to be of great benefit'. So, in other words, one is presenting a powerful rationale why this system should be used. However, one would also want to ask clients, for example, to 'complete the attached questionnaire which will provide us with a fuller picture of your current difficulties'.

Windy Dryden: For what purpose?

Michael Barkham: Twofold. One, having that kind of quantitative or qualitative information concerning people is part of the evaluative research which I think counselling psychologists should be adopting. Second, as a general strategy, I think one wants that information on the clients one is seeing. But this maybe modifies the open-endedness strategy slightly. I think one has to be aware of those clients who will be severely disturbed. One can still offer the model to them, but I think knowing this kind of information in advance is important.

Windy Dryden: Now, let's assume that I am going to offer the model to those people who don't meet the exclusion criteria. Will I then need to carry out a face-to-face assessment interview with these people?

Michael Barkham: One of the components of the model I spoke about earlier is 'therapy as assessment'; using the model with no prior face-to-face assessment.

Windy Dryden: So how do I assess?

Michael Barkham: Two points. First, by having prior information from the client, for example, self-report forms, quantitative or qualitative, which could be useful in terms of assessment. More important, perhaps, is the second point in which one used the therapy itself as assessment so that one is actually, in the initial part of the first session, getting down and focusing in with the client and saying 'What are the issues now that we feel we can address in the time we have available?'.

Windy Dryden: Let me be clear about this. Let's take the scenario where I am going to exclude clients by their responses to the questionnaires. I send out these assessment questionnaires first without mentioning the two-plus-one model; I get these forms back, I then assess them and select my clients. I then write to them and explain the two-plus-one model and ask for their informed consent. Then they come and we are underway. Am I correct?

Michael Barkham: Yes, you're off, straightaway.

Windy Dryden: Now, how can people get information concerning carrying out research into the model?

Michael Barkham: By reading papers [see 'Further reading' at the end of this interview] or by contacting me. My view is that one thing which has not facilitated research, and it equally applies to clinical and other areas, is the issue of having adequate resources. My view is that I would see myself as a resource on this in terms of collaboration, offering advice to people who want to evaluate both the model and their services in general.

Windy Dryden: That's very kind of you. Now, can the two-plus-one model be applied to any existing approach that counselling psychologists may use?

Michael Barkham: The bold answer is yes.

Windy Dryden: Do you have anything in mind which might lead you to give a more conservative response to this question?

Michael Barkham: At the moment, my position is that I think it is theoretically challenging to look at the core components of different theoretical models and see how they can be adapted and moulded into this particular service delivery model.

Windy Dryden: What do I need to do to adapt my approach to the model? What advice would you give on this point?

Michael Barkham: My advice would be to go back and look at the theoretical model of counselling that one is working in and, either by clinical hunch or by research evidence if there is any, pull out the core components of the particular therapeutic modality. You see, one of the academic rationales for the model which I mentioned right at the very beginning derives from our concern to address the 'equivalence paradox', that is, that very different therapies have broadly similar outcomes. By offering a very brief, high-impact and technically driven mode of delivery, one is minimising what have been termed in the literature the 'non-specifics' or 'common' factors which may contribute to the equivalent findings; what is being presented instead is specific to a particular theoretical model of delivery. So, in response to your question, it is a matter of identifying what those technically specific components of the therapeutic model are, and then structuring the delivery around those components.

Windy Dryden: Now let me play devil's advocate for the moment. It seems to me that using the two-plus-one model really does encourage one very strongly to be efficient in one's use of therapy time. It thus encourages the practitioner to be quite active. Now, if I was one of many counselling psychologists and counsellors who would view taking an active–directive stance with scepticism, on the one hand, to outright horror, on the other, how would you reassure me that taking an active–directive stance isn't horrific? I can imagine that's how some people are going to respond particularly those who are used to giving clients a lot of time and space to explore their concerns.

Michael Barkham: And my role, as counsellor, is to sit here and listen to the client.

Windy Dryden: And to work at their own pace, not to get them to work at my pace, which is basically what you are asking them to do. It comes back to the question of fitting the client to the model versus adapting the model to the client. But it does seem to me that the practitioner using this model does need to be active and directive and I can see that turning off hordes of counselling psychologists.

Michael Barkham: Right, well let's take one aspect of counselling, for example, listening or giving the client space to tell their story, which may be a core component for the theoretical model adopted by many counselling psychologists. I suppose one can take two stances. First, one could say 'OK, what would happen if I was more active?', and test that out, because giving the client the message that I am actually listening is not just about giving them space, it's about hearing accurately what they are saying and feeding back to them and developing a conversation in that kind of way. The second strategy would be to say, 'OK, for this first session I am going to let the client tell their own story at his or her pace and give them as much of the session as they want because that is, theoretically, the core component of the model of therapy that I deliver.'

Windy Dryden: That is an active ingredient in other words.

Michael Barkham: So I am going to use that in that kind of way, but then towards the later part of the session clearly pull in and say 'What have you got from that; how has that actually progressed us in our understanding your problem?'. In some way it is not left there; it is actually utilised and in a way that would be theoretically challenging. Is it, as you said, that listening is a sufficiently active ingredient to deliver the goods to the client? It's an empirical question.

Windy Dryden: I can see this model being more easily adopted by advocates which in the Sheffield project you call 'prescriptive', that is, who already advocate activity and directiveness on the part of the therapist.

Indeed, even Bob Hobson's conversational model which would come under the broad heading of what you call the 'exploratory' approach is quite active and directive. However, I can still imagine counsellors who, although they would hear what you have to say concerning the importance of trying out the model and testing its efficacy, would say: 'That's all very well, but I have developed my approach over many years; I have a lot of clinical experience now which shows me that it is important for me not to be that focused or active–directive, so quickly. I can understand perhaps in the middle stage of counselling that I can usefully become more focused but you are asking me to truncate much more than I desire in the initial period of counselling. You are asking me to rush and not allow for the gradual unfolding of a relationship where the client is encouraged to tell their story in their own way and at their own pace, where I stay with any silences that develop etc.'

Michael Barkham: Yes, I hear that and I agree. I would understand people holding that particular view. I think that raises a number of issues, not least that I think any counselling psychologist is only as good a practitioner as the extent to which he or she feels comfortable in the model in which he or she works. I would not advocate people adopting this model, or any other model, in which they did not feel comfortable.

Windy Dryden: Right, so we have talked about exclusion criteria for clients with respect to the model. Maybe we should look at exclusion criteria for counselling psychologists.

Michael Barkham: Yes, but I think what is interesting about that is that it raises a moral issue about whether counselling psychologists should be placing exclusion criteria on any service delivery system to clients. For example, that may be their preferred model but the whole notion of counselling is that it is there for the client.

Windy Dryden: Right. I think that is exactly what these people would say, that this model is in a sense not 'there' for the client. They would claim that they adapt their approach to their clients by working actively with some and more slowly with others. They would say that it is you that is not being 'client-centred' in the broad meaning of that term if they were to debate with you on this issue.

Michael Barkham: Right, but I think that is a debate that is worth having because I think that those kind of assumptions need to be challenged and tested and, ultimately, if they do not hold up, if in fact counselling psychologists find that clients don't benefit from it and they can't themselves as therapists work in that mode, then clearly the model in that set of circumstances hasn't a lot going for it. But it seems to me that it is challenging for counselling psychologists to say, 'Well, if my view is actually to provide something for the client', and I come back to the terms you used like 'unfolding', 'taking time' etc., 'in the back of my mind I am thinking of all those people out there who are waiting and can't get anything while all this "time" is unfolding'.

Windy Dryden: Right. If I am a counselling psychologist in private practice, I don't have a problem with waiting lists, my problem is likely to be the opposite, that I don't have enough clients. Why on earth should I implement the two-plus-one model under these circumstances?

Michael Barkham: Well, you're raising the thorny issue of finances. I think one has an obligation to the client, particularly if they are paying, to provide them with the most efficient service, and it may sound a bit 'hard-headed' but in a way, as a consumer, they have as much right to go round 'shopping' for good value as they would for any other commodity. I think counselling psychologists owe it to themselves that if in fact they are spending a longer period delivering that service to clients, they should know that it is, for these clients, the most effective and efficient mode to offer. So I am not advocating that everything should be shorter *per se*, but rather that people should have an empirical basis upon which to support their views.

Windy Dryden: OK, just let me sum up. The two-plus-one model has been developed mainly in response to growing waiting lists in the health service, but not exclusively so. It is derived from an evidential base, although you recognise that other versions of similar models could also be derived from that base. It has been developed partly so that you can study the process of psychotherapy. It has wide applicability. I would say that it is perhaps even more applicable to the work of counselling psychologists than clinical psychologists because it is likely to be of more help to people who are not severely disturbed and who don't have multiple difficulties. The model seems to throw out a challenge to counselling psychologists in a number of ways. First, it is saying, look you are a counselling psychologist and this has been devised from an evidential base, you can't easily dismiss it, so test it out, but test it out while doing research on it. It also encourages people to examine or perhaps re-examine some sacred cows. For example, you may believe that it is quite important to spend three, four or five sessions encouraging clients to be comfortable in a counselling situation, to talk at their own pace, but the research literature challenges that, so again it is encouraging counselling psychologists to look at their cherished ideas and realise that maybe those cherished ideas don't have much good research evidence in support of them.

   So it is challenging in a number of ways, it seems to me, and you are not just issuing these challenges to people without providing support because you have said that anybody who is interested in this model, or evaluation in general, should contact you. Is that an accurate summary of what we have discussed?

Michael Barkham: Yes, that is well summarised.

Further Reading

BARKHAM, M. (1989a). Brief prescriptive therapy in two-plus-one sessions: Initial cases from the clinic. *Behavioural Psychotherapy* 17, 161–175.

BARKHAM, M. (1989b). Exploratory therapy in two-plus-one sessions: I–Rationale for a brief psychotherapy model. *British Journal of Psychotherapy* 6, 81–88.

BARKHAM, M. (1989c). Towards designing a cost-effective counselling service: Lessons from psychotherapy research and clinical psychology practice. *Counselling Psychology Review* 4, 24–29.

BARKHAM, M. and HOBSON, R. F. (1989). Exploratory therapy in two-plus-one sessions: II – A single case study. *British Journal of Psychotherapy* 6, 89–100.

BARKHAM, M. and SHAPIRO, D.A. (1988). Psychotherapy in two-plus-one sessions: A research protocol. SAPU Memo 891. Department of Psychology, University of Sheffield.

BARKHAM, M. and SHAPIRO, D.A. (1989). Towards resolving the problem of waiting lists: Psychotherapy in two-plus-one sessions. *Clinical Psychology Forum* 23, 15–18.

BARKHAM, M. and SHAPIRO, D.A. (1990a). Exploratory therapy in two-plus-one sessions: A research model for studying the process of change. In: G. Lietair, J. Rombauts and R. Van Balen (eds), *Client-centred and Experiential Psychotherapy in the Nineties*. Leuven: Leuven University Press.

BARKHAM, M. and SHAPIRO, D.A. (1990b). Brief psychotherapeutic interventions for job-related distress: Pilot cases in prescriptive and exploratory therapy. *Counselling Psychology Quarterly* 3, 133–147.

BARKHAM, M., MOOREY, J. and DAVIS, G. (1992). Cognitive–behavioural therapy in two-plus-one sessions: A pilot field trial. *Behavioural Psychotherapy* 20, 146–153.

MARKMAN, P., MILLS, H. and BARKHAM, M. (1989). Hero innovators at home: developing co-operative research within a district clinical psychology department. *Clinical Psychology Forum*, 23, 19–22.

RIORDAN, J., WHITMORE, R. and BARKHAM, M. (1989). Less talk: More action. *The Health Service Journal* 99, 1164.

Chapter 4
Counselling under Apartheid

An Interview with Andrew Swart

Andrew Swart is currently the Head of the Counselling and Careers Unit at the University of the Witwatersrand, Johannesburg, which he joined in 1981. He comes from a 'white' liberal, English-speaking South African family located in a conservative, mainly Afrikaner, farming community in the Northern Transvaal. Witnessing apartheid from this perspective served, over time, to deepen his abhorrence and rejection of the system.

After several different jobs, he settled into education and taught in private schools for 14 years. During this time he studied by correspondence with the University of South Africa, obtaining a BA in philosophy and English, a Higher Education Diploma and an honours degree in clinical and counselling psychology. In 1977 he moved with his family to London, where he worked in the social services before completing a postgraduate diploma and a master's degree in the psychology of education at the Institute of Education, University of London. He then served an internship in South Africa, and registered as a counselling psychologist in 1983.

Living and studying in London and then working as a student counsellor at Witwatersrand extended and transformed his sociopolitical views and especially his awareness of the political roles of educational systems and of counselling. The following interview took place in August, 1989.

Windy Dryden: I would like to begin by asking you to talk about some of the pressures that counsellors working in South Africa face today.

Andrew Swart: There are a variety of pressures and I would like to classify these in the following way: first, there are structural pressures that relate to professional issues and, second, there are pressures that counsellors are subjected to in their personal lives and in their interaction with clients. I would like to say at the outset that pressure only becomes stressful when it is perceived to be stressful. So a lot depends upon counsellors' own social and political perspectives, concerning whether or not they are aware of the contexts of problems affecting their clients.

Windy Dryden: Which type of pressure would you like to address first?

Andrew Swart: The pressure which arises from personal interaction with clients. The first point that I would like to make is that there is a high general level of stress among individuals in South Africa, so I believe that counsellors do see a fairly large number of people who are highly stressed and upset. More specifically, counsellors who work in the 'open' universities or in the black or coloured communities of South Africa see a large number of young people and older people who have been traumatised by South African society.

For example, a student, who had been apparently randomly detained by the security police, comes to mind. This person had not been politically active and had been deliberately avoiding political activity. However, due to unexplained circumstances which occurred during a security police raid, he was detained for 60 days in solitary confinement, and after he was released, he came for counselling. I was confronted with the sense of outrage and the trauma that this person had been subjected to. This put pressure on me, because what should I, as a professional, do about something that is so blatantly unjust? Do I just treat the person and help him to work through his feelings of outrage and encourage him (or her) to cope more or less normally, or do I take the matter further? It raises uncomfortable questions of professional ethics and personal interest.

This moves us directly into the structural question, where counsellors have to decide whether or not to confront the repressive system which apartheid is, and which results in such personal violations. To do so is to take a political stand. One could more easily take up more 'professional' issues where the system of the security forces flagrantly violate professional ethics. Thus, for instance, a couple of colleagues have had to tolerate the presence of security forces sitting in on their interviews to ensure that nothing subversive was discussed between counsellor and client. This does not often happen, but when it does I think that it is intolerable.

Windy Dryden: So the first kind of pressure concerns the extent to which you deal with the distress of a client without in effect trying to intervene directly to do something about the societal origins of the distress. How have you and your colleagues tackled the issue of direct intervention?

Andrew Swart: We have tried to intervene on several levels. First, we have looked at our practice as counsellors in the counselling unit here. We have tried to devise approaches to group and community counselling where one would create the conditions in which a group or community can address the common problems that its members face. In the example I gave you, where we became aware of security force personnel sitting in on counselling interviews, we drafted a resolution through our Society for Student Counselling in South Africa (SSCSA) to present to the relevant minister of law and order, protesting against this violation of professional ethics. This caused considerable discussion among the members of the society, some of whom thought that this repressive action was justified in order to protect the country from what they perceived to be an external aggressor.

Windy Dryden: So are you saying that these members would not regard letting security force personnel sit in on counselling interviews as a breach of confidentiality?

Andrew Swart: No, they would regard it as a breach of confidentiality, but they would argue that it is justified on the grounds of a higher-order need to protect the national security of the country. In such circumstances their position would be that individual rights can be violated in order to protect group rights.

Windy Dryden: What proportion of the membership of the Society of Student Counselling do you think held that view?

Andrew Swart: We discovered that it was the minority, because the matter was put to a vote and our complaint was upheld. Since then, I think that this minority has grown even smaller. More and more people have begun to realise that you have to protect individuals' rights. If you allow the state to violate individuals' rights, then where do you draw the line? It becomes an ethical question. As supposedly caring professionals, our primary obligation is towards the individual. But obviously there is also a wider social responsibility. One needs to analyse critically the reasons for state repression to see whether it really is in the interests of the majority of individuals.

Windy Dryden: So counsellors within the society were able to mobilise themselves and come up with an organised response against the violation of individuals' rights and against unprofessional practice. Let's look more closely at the Society for Student Counselling. How active has it been at looking at wider issues and problems in South Africa?

Andrew Swart: There had been a tendency for many years for the society to be quite inward-looking. The problems we considered at our conferences mainly concerned issues of technique and intervention. We seemed deliberately to avoid any reference to the educational crisis in this country and the turmoil in students' lives by labelling those things as 'political' and therefore none of our business.

Windy Dryden: So I guess some of you were faced with a choice of either colluding with the denial or bringing the issue out into the open.

Andrew Swart: That's right. Some of us felt that we had gone along with decisions not to confront important issues, for the sake of conviviality: like what was happening to students on campuses that had been taken over by the military, or what was happening in school disturbances in Soweta, for example, in 1976 and the early 1980s. But first, in order to see whether or not we were correct in our assumption that the society had in fact been avoiding such issues, two of my colleagues (Dr N. Cloete and Ms S. Pillay) did a retrospective analysis of the papers that had been presented at the society's annual conference and discovered that nothing contentious had ever really been discussed.

We also learned that a paper that had been written in English by an Afrikaans-speaking colleague was not accepted because it was written in English when he could have written it in Afrikaans. That decision revealed an implicit political bias. The reasons for rejecting the paper were apparently not because of its lack of academic or professional merit, but because of the language in which it was written.

So in 1986 we confronted the society in a paper. There we presented a speculative but carefully considered framework to explain psychologically what had happened, together with our analysis of past papers read at annual conferences. We referred to the particular incident I have just mentioned and also looked at the composition of the executive committee of the society to demonstrate that it had been controlled mainly by white Afrikaner males. We suggested that the society was implicitly colluding with the Afrikaner Nationalist government. This paper caused considerable controversy and was debated heatedly over two days during tea breaks and cocktail parties and in a special additional session.

Windy Dryden: Why do you think it took so long for the confrontation to take place?

Andrew Swart: My guess is that for a long time no one wanted to or dared to disturb the group cohesiveness of the dominant group which had been built up within the society. Also, we are often unaware consciously of implicit motives. We are embedded in myths. Speaking personally, I was new to the counselling field, and it took several years for me to realise the implicit political nature of any social intervention. In fact, at the first conference of the society that I attended, I in my naïvety criticised a counsellor from the South African Defence Force for wanting us to take a political stance by urging university and Technikon counsellors to smooth the way for graduates going into military service. He argued from research that the South African Defence Force had more problems with graduates than it had with matriculants, and that counsellors could play a very valuable role in counteracting some of the prevailing values on campus that were antagonistic to military service, largely because the SADF is used to support the apartheid state. I was the only counsellor there to challenge him. He did not consider his paper to be implicitly political. I felt very vulnerable because I didn't know whether or not I was on sure ground. It was interesting for me to learn afterwards that there was quite a lot of support for my view.

So I think that people tend to shy away from confronting authorities, especially when those authorities are very powerful and violent. The consequences of such confrontation can be very painful in some cases. Several of my counselling colleagues have been threatened, physically assaulted or detained. Earlier this year a member of the academic staff at this university (David Webster) was assassinated. It seems quite clear that it was a political assassination and I think a lot of people are frightened of that. Until one comes to terms with that kind of danger, either of social exclusion or physical danger, one tends not to take a positive stance against injustice.

Windy Dryden: That brings us on to a question which applies throughout the world, but let's focus on South Africa. The question is to what extent are counsellors in South Africa agents of change or to what extent do they help to perpetuate the political ideas of the government?

Andrew Swart: That is an issue that we have been thinking a lot about for a couple of years. I feel that counsellors can work in a reactive way and actually prevent change. I know of some colleagues, for example, who do not want the political situation in this country to change because they say they fear black majority rule. They may consider apartheid to be unjust, but they are prepared to tolerate its injustices in order to 'safeguard' their own future and that of their children. These counsellors are naturally white but not necessarily exclusively Afrikaners.

Then I think there is a large majority of counsellors who are politically passive and work quite happily within the system without questioning it, probably experiencing relatively little stress. But the state also supports them in confining their roles. It is in their interests not to rock the boat. Many such counsellors are politically unaware or, I think, naïve, and need to be actively confronted with the ubiquitous nature of political influence. For example, at the end of 1988 we ran a political awareness workshop at the annual conference of the Society for Student Counselling. This was attended by about 20 counsellors of various political persuasions and from different 'population groups'. The effect was dramatic. Everyone left the workshop completely convinced that politics has a pervasive influence on the lives of their clients and on their own lives. Previously many had denied this or had not been aware of how pervasive an influence it had been. People don't change unless they are challenged, I think: unless they have experiences which contradict their dominant perceptions. So I think that relatively few counsellors in South Africa work as agents of change.

Windy Dryden: Perhaps we can look at the issue of counsellors as agents of change at a local level. What is the Counselling and Careers Unit doing that might be regarded as a good model of counsellors as change agents?

Andrew Swart: We have tried to intervene at several levels but it has not been easy to put our ideas into practice; even to agree on policy. At the individual level, some of us have tried to help individual clients to unravel and understand the social and political forces that are impinging upon them when this has been relevant. We have attempted to make some clients aware of the links between their problems and the social and political conditions of life in which they find themselves. In some cases, I suspect that our clients are more politically aware than we are, and then we need to be open to their views if we are to be of help. We aim to encourage clients to realise that they may not be able to solve certain problems unless they join with other like-minded people who have similar problems so that they can address these problems together. As such, we have tried to move towards what we call a Social Action Programme or a Community Counselling Programme, where we hope to help people with similar problems create a common identity and a common understanding of the nature and causes of their problems, and hopefully to translate this into positive group action. We are still struggling to get this programme going.

Windy Dryden: Can you say a little bit about the form in which such social and community action takes place.

Andrew Swart: It takes several forms. Our primary obligation is to our own university community, and we have, for example, worked in one of the residences. Here we have tried to create a common understanding of the problems and tensions that exist within the residence which is roughly half black, half white, as well as male and female, and to encourage the students to try and solve these problems in collaboration with the residence staff. Also, if students come to visit us and reveal recurring problems with particular departments or with the university administration, we would contact the relevant people and say that we had seen a significant number of students with a particular problem and encourage them to see it as a structural problem. Very often staff have not been aware of the problem or they have not thought of it in terms which could solve the problem. They may have attributed or located the problems in the students themselves, labelling the students as troublemakers for example, instead of taking responsibility for a systematic problem. We have also been looking at the possibility of empowering students themselves to confront administrative and social structures which serve to perpetuate their problems.

In addition, many of my colleagues go out into the wider community and speak in schools, for example, providing relevant information about tertiary education and courses available. I myself have spoken to associations of guidance teachers, trying to make them aware of the fact that if they are working at the interface between the individual and society, then they have a political role. I feel that it is important that counsellors should be consciously aware of the political nature of their roles and of the ethical questions this raises.

Windy Dryden: What has been the institutional response to such activities?

Andrew Swart: At senior levels it has been very supportive because I think that the university really has an intent to change to a truly non-racial, non-discriminatory policy and has consistently adopted an anti-apartheid stance; but it is caught between different constituencies, which leads to ambiguity and inconsistency. It seems impossible to escape from the apartheid system if one lives in South Africa, but one needs to investigate and explore how one is colluding with the system before one can try to escape the system or change it. When we have explored this implicit collaboration and it has been made explicit, the university authorities have consistently supported our efforts. It has, I hope, also contributed to the general empowerment of the university as an agent of constructive change. But we in the CCU are still caught in these same conflicts between the constituencies which have different interests in the university and in career counselling.

Windy Dryden: However, I guess that there are universities and other institutions of education in South Africa that would not be supportive of counsellors as agents of change.

Andrew Swart: That's right. This is where we have to accept that there may be a point where the Society for Student Counselling which supposedly represents the interests of student counselling in South Africa may have to split if fundamental principles have to be compromised to enable it to remain whole. Some of us from universities which are committed to change have already looked at the possibility of splitting and forming alternative, competing associations. If you look at the history of professional associations in this country, it is very clear that this has been happening especially over the last decade or so. We have had similar problems with the Psychological Association of South Africa where an alternative association called the Organisation of Appropriate Social Services of Southern Africa (OASSSA) comprising mainly psychologists who are against apartheid was formed in reaction to PASA's sociopolitical insensitivity. Earlier this year there was a conference at the University of Western Cape, and although no formal body was constituted, it was publicised as a conference for psychologists against apartheid. It was attended mainly by black and socially active white psychologists, but very few, if any, psychologists who supported the government were present.

Windy Dryden: What are the implications of such splits for the world of counselling in South Africa?

Andrew Swart: Personally, I think that there is a lot to be said to prevent such splits, provided again that one is not compromised in fundamental ways. The longer we can continue communicating with each other, the more likely it is, I think, that constructive change will be brought about. I have faith that if people are confronted with injustices and are not able to conceal these with socially convenient myths, they will usually work to effect change. But then confrontation is also important and the existence of alternative organisations does present such a challenge. I think therefore that it's important to continue discussing these issues, to continue the process of understanding, to confront injustice, and to confront each other respectfully. If we do split then communication easily breaks down. However, if it does come to the point where those of us who are committed to social change are not allowed to carry on such activities, or are significantly hampered, then I think we will split and we will carry on independently of the other body.

Windy Dryden: And that would be a sad day.

Andrew Swart: Yes, I think so. It would also be a sad day for many of those who disagree with people like me, who think we are too 'radical', because I think they also see the importance of communication and dialogue. It is significant that a couple of institutions immediately withdrew from the Society for Student Counselling and have remained outside it from the moment we confronted the society, because they said we were politicising it, which of course we are. On the other hand, people like me are also considered by some to be too compromising and not sufficiently radical.

Windy Dryden: I would like to shift the focus of our discussion slightly and introduce a personal note. When I was invited to come to South Africa to train groups of helping professionals comprising mainly psychologists in rational–emotive therapy (RET), that caused me a dilemma. I was clear that if the invitation had come from an official government body then I would have turned it down. However, as the invitation came from an independent group who assured me there would be a multiracial audience, I considered on balance that I would come. I would be interested to hear your view of the advantages and disadvantages of somebody like me, a British counsellor, coming to South Africa to train South African counsellors.

Andrew Swart: The advantages are that the open exchange of information and skills is, I believe, potentially to the benefit of all. However, the disadvantages are that if you were to have come to this country and trained reactionary or merely exploitative psychologists in skills, then it probably would not have been to the benefit of all. In other words, you could be empowering people to use skills to work against change or to exploit the status quo in a fairly manipulative way. I identify with the motivation behind the academic boycott and the general boycott against South Africa in its aim of bringing down the apartheid regime, but I am not sure about the effectiveness of it as a strategy. I fear that if a total academic boycott were imposed, it could do a lot of harm in disempowering those people in this country who are agents of change. It could also prevent the confrontation of people who are unsure, and even those who are conservative, with new ideas which could stimulate them to change.

How could we change without some outside stimulus? We would only change according to our own development. I do not negate the importance of our confronting our own problems, but we would be isolated from the additional benefit of international contexts and the stimuli of international perspectives. I would prefer to see a policy that has actually been recommended by a new association, the Union of Democratic University Staff Associations (UDUSA). UDUSA has taken over an alternative strategy of 'selective support' from the progressive medical organisation in South Africa. Rather than imposing a blanket ban on academic exchange, it suggests to the outside world that they should selectively support people who are in favour of meaningful change and who are working for such change. Internationally, it would support and encourage overseas visits by people who have a proven track record of attempting to change the society away from exploitation and racism and towards a democratic, non-racial and just society.

Windy Dryden: So, for somebody like me, the invitation I received was a risky one, because from what you are saying, I did not know in advance to what extent the counsellors that were coming to my workshops were reactionary, liberal or revolutionary. But what you are also saying is that you would encourage people from abroad to accept invitations that are issued by an organisation like UDUSA.

Andrew Swart: Yes, definitely, or OASSSA. UDUSA recently sent a delegation to the African National Congress, one of many delegations that have gone to consult with the ANC this year. The ANC said that it was satisfied with UDUSA's overall objectives and with its commitment to a democratic process in determining its policies.

Windy Dryden: What links would you like to see between counsellors in Britain and counsellors in South Africa?

Andrew Swart: I think that the time has come to collaborate on an international scale, because I see the ethical problems that we face in South Africa being reflected internationally. The South African government is blamed for its exploitation of black people. White people in South Africa are blamed for their racist exploitation in economic terms of black people, but I think that very little is done internationally to look at international exploitation of underdeveloped nations by developed nations. I think that counsellors working in areas like careers counselling and placement could look at the international implications of recruiting across countries. A specific example would be the recruiting of educated people from a developing country like South Africa to work in a country like England. There seems to me to be an exploitative aspect to that. But I also think it's a very valuable experience for South Africans to go and work in Britain, and I do believe that individuals should have the freedom to make such moves.

However, I think that there are international economic and political consequences which are hidden by myths prevalent in Britain, for example, as to its economic and political relationship in South Africa: that Britain doesn't exploit people like South Africa does. I believe that the exploitation is just less visible because it happens on another continent and at a higher, more abstract level.

So I would see counsellors having a socially activist role in Britain as well, encouraging British society to look not only at what you are doing to yourselves (e.g. minority groups, class differences) but what you are doing to other people in the world. British counsellors could benefit from being exposed to conditions in a developing country such as South Africa because of the stark and therefore more visible tensions here, and this might help them to understand their own country better. Hopefully this might foster more responsible action internationally.

Windy Dryden: So you would like to see some kind of job exchange?

Andrew Swart: Yes, that could be very useful in promoting fruitful dialogue and a common humanity.

Windy Dryden: One final question. When people think about South Africa, what comes immediately to mind is the political situation, and in this interview so far that has been a recurring, if not an ever-present, theme. To what extent do you think that such a focus obscures other issues that counsellors in South Africa are grappling with?

Andrew Swart: That is a very important question. I have been aware of the heavily political bias of the interview so far and also the focus on the symptoms of repression in this country, and that really forms a minor section of day-to-day work. Most of our work as counsellors is with mainly middle-class people who have common problems that exist all over the world. I think too strong a focus on the South African political situation might divert one from considering this fact.

Let me formulate this carefully. I think that sociopolitical issues affect all counsellors and their clients everywhere. But there are also other issues which may be more specific to South Africa, such as the authoritarian and multicultured nature of our society. When one has a diversity of authoritarian sociocultural systems coexisting, challenged by strong movements towards unitary, participative, non-racial democracy, individuals get caught in the interfaces of these competing social systems and can bring very complex problems to counsellors. For example, imagine the scope for problems in a hypothetical case of a young Christian Zulu woman coming from a conservative, traditional home, meeting and falling in love with a Muslim, Afrikaans-speaking 'coloured' fellow-student at a progressive university like Witswatersrand. We have quite a few cases of couples having problems with their families because of conflicting cultural values. Also, the alienation experienced by many individuals, I believe, is often dealt with by their identifying with like-minded groups into which they withdraw defensively.

This poses challenges to counsellors to work not only cross-culturally but in sociopolitically sensitive and aware ways. Most of our cultures put women in subordinate roles. And many black women find themselves at the bottom of the social pecking order in South Africa. Questions like what roles might men and women play in a post-apartheid South Africa, or the advantages and disadvantages of cultural differences, are important issues. But all of these issues I see as linked to sociopolitical contexts. As counsellors we are often not aware of the links, possibly because most of us are not trained to think in terms of the social systems influencing our clients and manifesting themselves as individual symptoms of distress.

Windy Dryden: To what extent do you think these issues that we have touched on – the political issues, the transcultural issues and the gender issues – are adequately looked at and dealt with on training courses for counsellors in South Africa?

Andrew Swart: I am not aware of well-developed training programmes for such issues. I think in recent years there has been a burgeoning awareness of them and I think that training courses do make some attempt in certain universities to look at them explicitly. Training courses are by no means uniform across South Africa, and a lot will depend on the sociopolitical perspective of the institution offering the training course. Some would not try to address the sociopolitical problems at all, preferring to see conflict as being purely between individuals, or cultural in nature, ignoring the economic links to race and class divisions. Everybody in South Africa, I think, especially the apartheid regime, regards the society as multicultural one. What one does about that multicultural society is a political issue that is at present being contested, and there is a very strong movement to transcend cultural differences and move towards a non-racial, democratic, unitary and just state. It sounds fine in the ideal. I hope we can achieve it, but there are considerable problems in doing so because of the plethora of hidden meanings and vested interests in the different sections of the South African population.

Windy Dryden: In this interview you have touched on your own feelings of optimism for the future of counselling in South Africa, although you have also mentioned the possibility of a split within the Society for Student Counselling. That certainly parallels my own experiences in talking with people in South Africa. There is a guarded optimism, but also a hidden fear that it could all come apart. So I find it interesting that this theme has been reflected in our interview as well.

Andrew Swart: I have often wondered whether that sense of optimism that I have also picked up and feel personally is based on reality, or whether it is a psychological defence mechanism against the possible disaster that faces this country. I have no doubt that the struggle is likely to be more violent than it has been up to now. Hopefully that violence will be short-lived, until we find a solution to our present problems, but I have a faith in the basic humanity of our people, in spite of the terrible damage suffered by both oppressors and oppressed. Counsellors, I believe, could play a vital role in facilitating constructive change and in healing some of the wounds.

Postscript by Andrew Swart (April 1990)

Much has happened since this interview took place in August 1989. President de Klerk's bold commitment to negotiate the dismantling of apartheid, the release of Mr Nelson Mandela and the unbanning of the ANC have taken South African politics into new areas and greater degrees of sophistication. Although most of us welcome these changes, the fundamentally important issues are still being contested. The established processes of authoritarian, divisive, exploitative and repressive government are not so easily changed, nor are their effects – to be seen in the widespread violence – so easily overcome.

In the SSCSA conference in October 1989, a clear and enthusiastic commitment to work proactively for a more humane and non-racist society emerged. But political differences as to what might constitute an acceptable structural basis for such a society were avoided. Perhaps this was in deference to the oft-expressed need for further communication and negotiation. The SSCSA is now in the process of reorganising itself structurally, to involve as many of its members as actively and as democratically as possible. Several working groups have been set up, including a standing Politics and Ethics Sub-Committee.

Numerous organisations are now urgently debating policies for post-apartheid mental health systems. Some are discussing what to do to help the estimated hundreds of thousands of exiles who have begun to return to South Africa. The ferment of issues is complex and challenging, and the feelings of optimism and of fear seem to be intensified.

Reading and editing the transcript of the interview made me realise that it represents only a partial and personal view. No reference was made to colleagues in the psychological profession other than student counsellors; to social and other health workers; to the important work done by organisations such as OASSSA; nor to what appears to be happening in the Psychological Association of South Africa and its various institutes, especially the Institute of Counselling Psychology.

Chapter 5
Therapist Sexual Abuse
An Interview with Jill Sinclair

Jill Sinclair coordinates the Support Network for those Abused by Therapists. She has published articles about therapist abuse and about her own personal experience of such abuse. She took part in a BBC television programme about abuse by therapists which was shown in 1990.

It was her own experience of sexual involvement with a therapist that led her to start the Network in 1989. She soon found that her own situation was far from unique, although until now there did not even appear to be a name given to what was going on.

Ignorance and secrecy about sexual abuse by therapists has led many to suffer in silence. The Network is an attempt to end the isolation and secrecy: to help each other talk about and share their experiences, give emotional support, share helpful information, form their own understanding and increase awareness generally.

Jill has brought up two children and a dog . . . She obtained an honours degree in English literature, from the New University of Ulster, as a mature student. Since leaving university she has worked in the book trade, but her interests have moved in the direction of psychology and personal growth, including the debunking of traditional psychoanalytic theory. At the moment she is doing research on the subject of therapist abuse. She also coedits a newsletter, *Threshold*, which is the publication of an organisation concerned with women and mental health. In spite of her exploitative experience, Jill feels very positive about the therapy she underwent for a year prior to it.

Windy Dryden: In this interview, Jill, we will be considering several issues concerning a topic that has been called various things. Terms that *you* prefer are 'therapist sexual abuse' or 'professional incest', although such behaviour has been termed, for example, 'role-inappropriate sexual behaviour'. Perhaps we could start by looking at why you prefer the terms 'sexual abuse' and 'professional incest', and why you dislike the terms 'role-inappropriate behaviour' or 'role-inappropriate sexual behaviour'.

Jill Sinclair: I think terms like 'role-inappropriate behaviour' are euphemisms and fudge over what is really happening. 'Role-inappropriate behaviour' could be something quite mild, and 'inappropriate' seems a very mild word to use for sexual abuse by therapists. It might be inappropriate for a therapist to make a spelling mistake in letters; it might be inappropriate to wear jeans for a therapy session; but 'inappropriate' doesn't describe the damage clients suffer from therapist sexual abuse. I believe the only word you can use to describe what is going on is *abuse*. We use the word abuse to describe parents having sex with their children. Not until we use the right *words* can people start to deal with what's happened.

Windy Dryden: What types of therapist behaviour do you consider merit the term 'sexual abuse'?

Jill Sinclair: There are lots of varieties and subtleties. It doesn't necessarily mean that the therapist has had sexual intercourse with a client. Some therapists don't even touch the client, but they can still cross the boundaries and turn it into something sexual. Some therapists will actually get clients to touch themselves, or will get clients to talk about sexual things and enjoy it in a voyeuristic way, or the therapist might touch the client and it will end up as mutual masturbation. There are lots of degrees of sexual exploitation that are just as harmful, as we are discovering in the field of child sexual abuse: it doesn't have to be actual intercourse.

Windy Dryden: You mentioned crossing the boundaries. I would like to explore that a little because in some approaches to counselling and psycho-therapy, physical contact – I guess what is called non-erotic physical contact, through hand-holding or hugging – is actually advocated. Where does one draw the boundary in this arena?

Jill Sinclair: I think that it's sad that some people can't understand the difference between physical contact and sex, assuming that when you are against sexual abuse in therapy, you're against touching. There's really something wrong with a therapist who doesn't understand the difference between physical contact and sexual contact. A lot of people think that the problem of sexual abuse is only because of the new therapies, where there's much more human contact than in the more traditional therapies. Some of the bodywork therapies are very physical as well, and include massage, for example.

But it's interesting that the research that has been done shows that abuse by therapists doesn't bear any relation to whether the therapy is physical or to the amount of physical access that the therapist has to the client. In fact, according to one study, the therapists who sexually exploit their clients most are the ones who work in the most formal settings: psychiatrists or clinical psychologists. I'm not saying it doesn't happen in the new therapies, but I don't think that is where the main problem lies. I would hate to see psychotherapy becoming very cold and clinical: it's like parents being told not to touch their children in case they might sexually abuse them.

Windy Dryden: One guideline for women in terms of the general area of sexual harassment has focused on the idea that 'it's harassment if it feels like harassment'. Would you like to see the same guideline being offered to clients in psychotherapy?

Jill Sinclair: Yes, definitely. The client *knows* when it's wrong. I knew exactly, on one level, when it wasn't therapy and when there was something wrong, and as soon as it crossed the boundary I felt ashamed. That was when I couldn't talk about it, not even to a friend. It was before anything which could be said to be 'proof' of sexual contact had taken place. I think you do know, even if on another level you are so desperate for the therapist's love that you go along with it. You know that you're being exploited.

Windy Dryden: Right, so can I attempt to paraphrase here? When physical contact is within the context of a therapeutic relationship, not in an abusing relationship, then it feels right on both sides and is therapeutic for the client. When the feelings of there being 'something not quite right here' start to bubble up into the client's consciousness, then that's an indication that the boundary has been crossed?

Jill Sinclair: Yes. Or if the client feels ashamed and it's something that they can't tell anybody about, then there's something wrong. For me, I knew I couldn't share it in a group. I think that if a therapist is worried about his or her feelings towards a client, then he or she shouldn't initiate physical contact in a private session. Maybe it's better to do it in a group, and then everybody feels comfortable about it.

Windy Dryden: Let's move on to look at the effects of sexual abuse on clients. What are the major effects of this kind of abuse?

Jill Sinclair: I think the effects can be likened to child sexual abuse. Going by my own experience, I would say it was the most traumatic experience of my life. It's an absolute, complete betrayal. There are so many things to say about that, that I hardly know where to start. I think that the damage it does and what it does to women's self-esteem has got to be recognised.

That's why the naming is so important. It must describe the reality so you have got something to confront. If you don't label the abuse as abuse, you go through trauma, but there's nothing to be angry at because you can't be angry if somebody has just behaved inappropriately or if it was your fault. With a lot of women it affects their sexual relationship: either they can't have sex, or some studies show women becoming more promiscuous as a result – it's as if you're programmed to think that's the only way you can get sex. For me, I haven't been able to have a sexual relationship since that happened. It's affected my relationship with my children, my friends, and it's affected my work – and I've heard that from *other* women, too.

Windy Dryden: Would you say that the effects are exacerbated because it's abuse by somebody who has hitherto been trusted?

Jill Sinclair: That's the whole thing: even for people who haven't been in therapy for very long. If you've agreed to deal with your feelings with somebody, you have to trust them. If you didn't trust them, you would go to somebody else. So, in my case, I'd built up a lot of trust because I'd been doing successful therapy for about ten months. Some people have been in therapy for many years before it develps into a sexual relationship, and they have developed incredible trust in, and respect for, their therapist. In that case, it really is like incest. It isn't like an ordinary relationship that you might have outside. In a way the therapist is keying into and exploiting primal feelings and needs, including hope of parental love.

Windy Dryden: What forces do you think exist in the therapeutic situation that really make it hard for women – and it is mainly women who have been abused as clients – to prevent them from terminating this relationship?

Jill Sinclair: Most of those I've spoken to have found it difficult to get out of the relationship, even when they have become more and more distressed. I've heard of women who have gone even more downhill and have got worse and worse. Their friends have noticed and have been unable to help them. For *me* it was incredibly hard to get out. I was driven to the point of suicide before I was actually able to leave, because I couldn't let go of my therapist and I was confused. I was caught up in all this emotional mess. My therapist had offered me something, so I kept going back to try and work it out. I didn't want to be rejected; I didn't want to just walk away, I suppose. That would have meant losing my therapy and losing my *therapist*. I think some therapists abruptly stop the relationship, and that's really hurtful because it's a terrible rejection for the client. They probably find that the relationship has become a nuisance or an embarrassment for them.

Windy Dryden: Before we look at what advice you have for clients who feel that they may be in an abusing relationship with their therapist, there is some scant evidence which shows that having sex with a therapist can have a positive relationship on a very small minority of clients. For example, a paper written by Janice Russell (1990) refers to a woman in this way: 'It is notable at this point that the woman who found intimate physical contact both appropriate and constructive differed in three identical ways from the other respondents. Firstly, she and her therapist were of the same gender; secondly, she was the respondent who was still in the therapeutic relationship in question; and finally, she felt strongly that the physical contact, which was initiated at her request, was fulfilling *her* needs and not those of the therapist.' Every stage of therapy was talked through together and negotiated so that she understood the physical contact was a means to an end not an end in itself. And Russell goes on to quote the respondent thus:

'I'm using her sexually, she is not using me. There's been clear boundaries and limitations from her, even when there wasn't from me fantasy wise' (p. 48). What's your view on the evidence that, in rare instances, having sex with a therapist can have a positive impact on a client?

Jill Sinclair: Well, I don't want to deny what anybody says about his or her experience, but I think it's very dangerous to give the impression that it could be a good idea. One thing is that sometimes, as women, we seem to idealise relationships with other women. We don't want to think that women can sexually abuse in the same way as men. We don't want to think that mothers can sexually abuse, and sometimes we're in danger of saying it's abusive if men do it but if women do it it's much more positive. I'm a bit confused about the point the respondent made about talking through every stage of the therapy, because it *isn't* therapy. That woman has gone to therapy not to have a sexual relationship, which she can have outside, but to deal with her feelings.

Instead of dealing with her feelings, she's had a sexual relationship with her therapist. So what's happened to the feelings she has gone into therapy to deal with? And even if the therapist is a woman, the same gender as the client, there's no way it's an equal relationship like you have outside. She initiated the sexual contact with the therapist, but was it in a therapy session?

It seems irresponsible to me that a therapist can respond even to that initiation. The respondent says there were 'clear boundary limitations' from the therapist, but how can the therapist be clear about boundaries if she actively particpates in her client's fantasies? She isn't really doing her client any favours. It's just not a good idea to give the impression that it can be a positive experience. The founder of the re-evaluation co-counselling movement, Harvy Jackins, had a similar point to make about the co-counselling relationship, which is as democratic as you can get in therapy. He said he has never heard of one good relationship emerging from a co-counselling relationship which turned into a sexual relationship. He says that it's just not possible.

Windy Dryden: Do you think in the example that I quoted that it's telling that the respondent was still in the therapeutic relationship, and that perhaps after the relationship has ended she may come to re-evaluate that experience and realise that it may have been abusive?

Jill Sinclair: Yes. If you talk to people while they are still in a sexual relationship with their therapist, they are high on feelings, or in a confusion of feelings. I wouldn't have called it sexual abuse while it was happening to me. I wouldn't even have recognised it as applying to me, and it's not until years and years later that I gradually started to see how things really were, when I had extricated myself from the emotional involvement. And I've heard of the same thing happening to other women.

Windy Dryden: Let's move on to the work that you have done since your own experience. I believe that you were responsible for setting up the Support Network for those Abused by Therapists*. Could you say a little bit about what prompted you to establish this network and also something of its work?

Jill Sinclair: What prompted me to set it up was that I wanted to find other women who had the same experience so that I didn't feel so isolated. It made a lot of difference finding somebody else who understood. I started off finding a few women to talk to, and it was really good. This was about the time when Peter Rutter's (1990) book came out, which attracted quite a lot of publicity. So I put something in *The Guardian* which got quite a good response from people all over the country, even somebody in Russia and another one in France. That's how the Network started, and it is growing all the time. I meet up with people if possible, correspond with some, circulate information, and send out booklists, press cuttings and anything else I think might be useful. I put people in the same area in contact with one another, and people who are going through a complaints procedure can be put in contact with others who have already gone through such a procedure.

It is self-help, and aims to share experiences, raise awareness, do research, provide educational material for professionals and professional organisations, and get the legal system to recognise this form of abuse. Moreover, it aims to develop strategies for dealing with abusing therapists and to develop an understanding of our own and others' needs after this kind of abuse. Theories that label us are not helpful: rather, every person's experience is unique to her or him.

At the end of March we had a meeting in Brighton where the Support Network met with the local therapeutic community to hear Peter Rutter give a talk and have a discussion. This was very successful: over 70 people came and it was good to see the number of professionals now interested. I was also pleased to see students of counselling and psychology present at the talk.

Windy Dryden: How would you like to take this issue further?

Jill Sinclair: What I would like to see is more practical help for people who have been sexually abused by their therapist and want some help. I think that one useful thing would be for clients to have advocates, so that if they want to confront the therapist, they have support. Lots of people actually want to confront their therapist and want the therapist to admit that they have done something wrong. They want to have their harm acknowledged, and at the moment the only way to do that is by going through a whole complaints procedure. Even if you are willing to go through the courts and even if the complaint is upheld, which is highly unlikely, it's a

* Support Network for those Abused by Therapists, PO Box 542, North Road, Brighton BN1 1AA.

dreadful process to go through. It might be more satisfactory in some cases for a client to go with an advocate to the therapist and to confront the therapist. They can then get the therapist to pay for subsequent therapy, and to refund the client for what she's already paid for the therapy, as a recognition that the client has been harmed. I think that's really important.

Windy Dryden: In terms of situations where a client who has been in an abusing relationship with the therapist seeks help from a new therapist, what is needed from this new therapist? What does the new therapist have to take into account in terms of helping that person?

Jill Sinclair: Sometimes people go to a therapist who is actually known to their original therapist. If the therapist *is* a colleague of the abusing therapist, or in any way connected socially, it is very difficult to be unbiased. It can just cause more problems. It's safer if a therapist doesn't work with a client when he or she knows the therapist who abused the client, because you often find that the second therapist tries to protect the abusing therapist: a sort of 'keep it in the family' situation arises.

Windy Dryden: OK, let's assume that the new therapist doesn't know the abusing therapist. What is needed from the new therapist in terms of approach in helping the abused client?

Jill Sinclair: They need a lot of patience, and they should think beforehand: Have I got the patience and the stamina to take this person on? For one thing, they might get involved in a legal procedure: they have to be willing to go through that. For another thing, it takes such a long time to build up trust. It's so difficult for someone abused by one therapist to build up trust with another. The one essential thing for the client is that you are believed without any doubt whatsoever. If they don't believe the client, then I don't think they should take her or him on. So it's most beneficial for the therapist to believe the client absolutely and to reiterate that the abuse wasn't the client's responsibility: that it was 100% the therapist's responsibility.

Windy Dryden: You mentioned the importance of patience. What therapeutic issues come up again and again that the new therapist would have to be patient in seeing through?

Jill Sinclair: Abused clients are likely to be very suspicious. They may be desperate for help, but just don't want to open up, and feel very frightened of being used again in any way. Subsequent therapists shouldn't go behind the patient's/client's back, speaking to another therapist or doctor, making arrangements or telling somebody about the abuse when they haven't asked permission. To do things like that can be so damaging, yet I've heard of cases where subsequent therapists have made just such mistakes.

Windy Dryden: Doing so is a further betrayal of trust?

Jill Sinclair: It's a further betrayal, and it takes away the client's autonomy when that's what really needs to be built up. It has taken away your control again. The new therapist has to be so sensitive.

Windy Dryden: Let's move on to how you would like to see the profession of counselling and psychotherapy respond to therapist sexual abuse. Perhaps we could start off by looking at the latest version of the BAC Code of Ethics and Practice for Counsellors, which has the following item: 'Counsellors must not exploit their clients financially, sexually, emotionally, or in any other way. Engaging in sexual activity with the client is unethical.' What do you think of the way the item is phrased?

Jill Sinclair: This has been changed from the previous code of ethics which I believe stated that sexual activity between counsellor and clients was *'usually'* unethical. I'm glad they have changed it to the unambiguous *'is'* unethical.

The only problem is that although it's good to have this code of practice and code of ethics written down, if therapists want to have a sexual relationship with their clients they can rationalise almost anything. Rutter (1990) cites therapists who decide to stop the therapy relationship so that they can have a sexual relationship with their client. They may stop the therapy halfway through one session, for instance, and say: 'Well we stopped the therapy relationship, so that's OK, we'll now start a sexual relationship.' I think that's a bit dodgy.

Windy Dryden: In America there are some states, I believe, where once you have had any kind of therapeutic contact with a client, then any kind of sexual relationship, no matter how long afterwards, is regarded as unethical. In other states, I believe, a time period of perhaps two years needs to elapse before any sexual activity is regarded as outside that realm of the unethical.

How would you like this code to be changed to deal with the fact that it still leaves open the fact that you can terminate the relationship and then have sex almost immediately with your client?

Jill Sinclair: There seems to be more awareness of this issue in the United States. In some states, for a therapist to have sexual contact with a client is not just unethical, but illegal. Maybe we need to consider it illegal here too.

Windy Dryden: You have written about your experience of being sexually abused by your therapist and some of the issues that arise from it (Sinclair, 1990). I would like to quote you because I think you raise an important issue. You say: 'Professional organisations have done a lot to contain this issue (namely therapist sexual abuse) and have a vested interest in "handling" complaints rather than investigating them and bringing to light anything that will rock the boat. . . . It seems that there's a whole conspiracy of silence which keeps knowledge of abuse in therapy hidden' (p. 9). Could you say a little bit more about that? For example, was it a result of your own or other people's experience that led you to this conclusion?

Jill Sinclair: It was a result of other people whom I have talked to. I have heard of people trying to make complaints. One that comes to mind is almost farcical: it's like the circumlocution office – she's just got a whole pile of paper and it just goes from one person to another person – but the professional involved will not accept responsibility and neither will the institution where he works. He continues working with just as much credibility.

It just seems so difficult for a client to be believed: any professional can just say that there is 'no proof'. And it seems that the higher you go up the hierarchy, the more you get fobbed off.

Even when it *is* taken seriously, it often seems to end up as a slight rap on the knuckles for the 'therapist': 'You made a bit of a mistake – promise not to do it again.'

Windy Dryden: How would you like to see professional organisations respond to complaints about therapist sexual abuse?

Jill Sinclair: At the moment they seem to be there for the protection of their members. I don't know whether they *can* represent clients, or whether clients need to be represented by somebody else. I would like to see corroborative evidence used as 'proof'. If more than one person is independently making a complaint against a therapist, shouldn't that be sufficient evidence? This corroborative evidence has been used by the General Medical Council as 'proof' against a doctor. To me that strengthens the evidence against the therapist. It is so often difficult to 'prove': it's not like being burgled or having bruises and scars. But if more than one person is saying it of the same therapist, then surely it should be taken really seriously.

Another thing I have heard of is that therapists are thrown out of one organisation and join another, and the second organisation doesn't actually know that they have already been excommunicated from the first. Perhaps there's a need for some kind of register of therapists that people can refer to and see which therapists have had complaints made against them. Some, of course, don't even belong to organisations.

Windy Dryden: I think that there *are* moves to start such a register now. There is the United Kingdom Standing Conference for Psychotherapy which has been set up to explore that issue.

Jill Sinclair: Can I say something about the UK Standing Conference for Psychotherapy? It is apparently a good idea, but saying that only people with the 'right' qualifications can practise won't of itself stop therapist sexual abuse, because therapists with 'good' qualifications are now sexually abusing their clients, and complaints aren't being processed – they aren't getting heard.

Windy Dryden: You seem to be hinting at the establishment of an independent panel or board that could investigate these complaints. Your worry, it seems to me if I have understood you, is when a professional organisation seeks to investigate claims against one of its members . . .

Jill Sinclair: It's like the police investigating the police. Well, we have ombudsmen, don't we, for other consumer matters, who are completely outside the organisation concerned. Maybe there could be an ombudsperson for therapy. Although it sounds contradictory, I also think that peer-group pressure is very important, where colleagues can keep an eye on each other, as in group supervision. I think that group supervision can be more effective in this respect than a hierarchical form of supervision where some people have so much authority that they can't be challenged.

Windy Dryden: Of course that does involve the offending therapist actually bringing that material to supervision, which I guess they will not be motivated to do.

Jill Sinclair: That's the problem, but in a group where therapists work together I think it would be difficult for it not to be noticed if a therapist was having late sessions or was having problems. I think it would be noticeable to other therapists. Perhaps if there were no hierarchy and no one was above criticism, it would be easier to bring up.

Windy Dryden: That brings us to the issue of how easy therapists would find it to confront their colleagues concering a suspicion of sexual abuse.

Jill Sinclair: I think that from what I've heard, therapists very rarely confront their colleagues. In my own experience they might have said, 'Look what you're doing, if this gets out there are going to be problems': a sort of 'keep it in the family' reproach.

Windy Dryden: Again the parallel would be with child sexual abuse: keep the secret within the family.

Jill Sinclair: That's right, and that's definitely not in the client's interest. Therapists say they can't do anything if you don't have cast-iron proof: it's like you have to go through the courts or something and have proof. They say we can't slander therapists, we can't say anything, if we don't have proof – but that's a kind of betrayal. Friends, for instance, have no problem believing that their friend is going through this distress and believing their stories, and yet professionals do seem to have a problem in this respect.

Windy Dryden: Finally, Jill, there has been some discussion, mainly in the American literature, on the rehabilitation of abusing therapists. Based on your own and other people's experiences that have arisen from the support network, what would you like to see involved in the rehabilitation of abusing therapists?

Jill Sinclair: I think that it would be good if therapists who have got caught in a sexual relationship, who are multiple abusers, want to get help, as long as there is somewhere for them to go. In America there is a walk-in counselling centre which is for both clients and therapists. In Britain, if abusing therapists want to do something about it, there's no chance for them, as there is nowhere for them to go. They have got to be able to work through their own feelings about it or they *will* just carry on doing it. But it would take an incredible lot of strength for a therapist to admit what they have been doing. If they've already got caught up in a sexual relationship with their client, they haven't demonstrated this strength. So I don't feel too optimistic that they would go and seek help, because it might ruin their career. I think that abusing therapists are dependent on what they're doing: they are already addicted to it. It would be incredibly difficult to admit what they are doing to themselves and to go and seek help. But there needs to be something there if they do.

Windy Dryden: In fact, one can even ask whether abusing therapists should be rehabilitated or perhaps encouraged or forced to leave the profession.

Jill Sinclair: I suppose you can make a parallel with child sexual abuse again. Once, say, a father has sexually abused his daughters, do you ever trust him again? I don't know whether I would. I don't know whether you could trust therapists who have sexually exploited their clients. Now I think about it, it would be difficult to do so. I can't imagine any client who knew that it had happened before actually choosing to go to such therapists, even if they had been rehabilitated.

Windy Dryden: On the other hand, a recent article by Palermo (1990) argues in favour of a compassionate, kind but just approach to the failing psychotherapist, as opposed to an excessively punitive action which would, he argues, mean that therapist be prevented from practising. Should abusing therapists be treated more harshly than perhaps clients who may themselves have abused their children sexually?

Jill Sinclair: If you are talking as a psychotherapist and identifying with psychotherapists, I can see you might advocate a nice, kind approach, but do we really want that? I mean: if a surgeon kept making mistakes, would we want him to carry on? You are trusting somebody with your feelings. To be kind to a therapist by saying 'You've made a mistake, try not to do it again', when he is leaving behind a trail of destruction, is not being very kind to the client or subsequent clients. We're not just talking about when your friend stands you up: we're talking about something really serious. I know of two women who have actually committed suicide because of it. Most of the women I've spoken to have said that they have been suicidal. So it seems that to say a therapist should be treated kindly, and be allowed to continue practising, is minimising what they're doing to these women.

Windy Dryden: To conclude on this issue, you wonder to what extent abusing therapists will come forward on their own initiative and admit to the abuse and seek rehabilitation. You seem to be saying: 'Look, this is *such* a betrayal of trust that we, as clients, really can't take the risk of having such therapists practise therapy.'

Jill Sinclair: If therapists come forward and admit it on their own, they may be genuine. But they may be doing so because they know they can't get out of it, so they think it's safer to come clean. I think we should consider seriously whether such therapists should be allowed to carry on doing therapy. And subsequent clients – shouldn't they know? If they did know, then surely they wouldn't choose to work with such a person.

References

PALERMO, G.B. (1990). On psychotherapist–patient sex: discussion paper. *Journal of the Royal Society of Medicine* 83, 715–719.

RUSSELL, J. (1990). Breaking boundaries: a research note. *Counselling: Journal of the British Association for Counselling* 1 (2), 47–50.

RUTTER, P. (1990). *Sex in the Forbidden Zone*. London: Mandala.

SINCLAIR, J. (1990). 'Breaking of Ethical Code'. *Sussex Counsellors' Newletter*, No. 23, 9–12.

Chapter 6
Dos and Don'ts and Sacred Cows
An Interview with Arnold Lazarus

Arnold Lazarus's contributions to psychotherapy have been immense. He has been at the forefront of developments in both behaviour therapy and cognitive–behaviour therapy and has pioneered a technically eclectic approach to clinical practice based on a thorough multimodal assessment of client problems.

Born in South Africa in 1932, Arnold Lazarus went to work in North America in the early 1960s where he has remained ever since. He is Distinguished Professor at Rutgers – The State University of New Jersey, a position he has held since 1972.

Throughout his career, Lazarus has made an active contribution to professional psychology. He has been elected President of several professional associations, has served on the editorial boards of 20 scientific journals, has been a consultant to numerous agencies, both public and private, and has fellowship status in several professional societies. He has received many honours for his contributions, most notably the 'Distinguished Service Award' from the American Board of Professional Psychology and the 'Distinguished Career Achievement Award' from the American Board of Medical Psychotherapists. He was also inducted into the National Academies of Practice in Psychology. He is listed in *Who's Who in America* as well as in *Who's Who in The World*. His 12 books and more than 150 journal articles and book chapters have led him to give invited addresses throughout the world. Several opinion polls have cited Arnold Lazarus as one of the most influential psychotherapists of the twentieth century.

In the interview that follows I discuss with Arnold Lazarus one of his most recent interests, namely challenging so-called received wisdom that has remained unquestioned by generations of psychotherapists.

Windy Dryden: One of your recent interests has been to develop a list of 'dos and don'ts' that have been passed down from generation to generation in the field of psychotherapy but have, by and large, remained un-challenged. Before we consider these in detail, could you say a little about how you became interested in this subject?

Arnold Lazarus: I found that most of my training consisted of being told what I was *not* to do. I was handed a long list of 'don'ts' and 'nevers' by my trainers and supervisors. Unfortunately, this is still true today in many

62

centres, where students are trained *never* to do this, *always* to do that, *not to* say that, and so forth. This runs counter to individual differences, to idiosyncratic needs, and undermines the uniqueness that people are all about. Now let me say at the outset, that there are a couple of absolute don'ts to which I subscribe. One of them is 'Don't engage in sexual contact with your clients'. This is not because I am a prude, but frankly I do not think that sex and therapy or counselling can mix. There are some clinicians who challenge that view, and have claimed that in fact positive gains have accrued when they have broken this taboo, but I am not willing to even entertain that because I think that the risks far outweigh the advantages. The risks here are those of exploitation, all kinds of false expectations, ambiguities, confusion of roles, and the violation of trust. So that certainly is one of my nevers and absolute don'ts. The other one is not to attack one's clients as human beings, that is not to put them down as people *in toto*, and avoid ridicule, scorn and derision. Would you like me to talk first about what I think some of the main mistakes are that therapists make that produce problems before we challenge some of the sacred cows?

Windy Dryden: Let's do that.

Arnold Lazarus: I think that there are some therapists who are noxious or destructive. Sometimes bad therapy is carried out by well-intentioned but poorly trained practitioners who apply incorrect techniques, or perhaps they apply the correct techniques, but do so poorly. But one of the destructive things that I think clinicians sometimes use are labels. They tell their clients that they have a passive personality, or a narcissistic personality disorder, and they use other labels that are very destructive. When therapists display disgust, disdain, impatience, blaming, disrespect, intolerance or induce guilt in their patients, this is when I think the most negative effects ensue. For example, if a therapist says 'Why didn't you wake up and do something before your son got hooked on drugs?', we have an example of a guilt-inducing statement, that is not meritorious in any sense. Or saying to a patient 'Well, you made a mess of that situation and now you expect me to pick up the pieces!' is only blaming the client and is of little (if any) help. These things happen more often than we want to believe. There are some therapists who are blatantly insensitive, and really ought to be in another field of endeavour.

When therapists are inaccurate, or when they fail to appreciate a client's feelings, or are highly inappropriate in timing their remarks, unfortunate consequences usually ensue. One of my clients reported that his previous therapist said, 'You have come a long way during the past eighteen months but if you terminate therapy now, you will be right back to square one before you know it'. Attempts to foster dependency are all too frequent. Not too long ago, there was an edition of the *New York Magazine*, where the cover had a person chained to an analyst's couch: the title was 'Prisoners of Psychotherapy' and the therapists interviewed anonymously said, 'Well, I hang on to patients as long as I can, because if somebody leaves me there is a gap in my appointment book and there goes my fee for the tennis club for that month, or my car payments suffer'. It is most unfortunate for people to be kept in therapy longer than they need to be. At a less damaging level we have instances of irrelevant questions, confusing remarks and false reassurance. It's just as bad to give false reassurance as it is to blame or condemn; you want to be honest with your clients. So those are some of the mistakes I think that therapists make and the public would be far better served if they did not make those kinds of mistakes.

But now let's get back to the first part of your question, and let me share with you some of the don'ts that I was given that I have now violated. They aren't in any particular order of importance. Let's start with one, which was *'Don't give advice'*. Now a lot of people assume that if you give advice you are somehow truncating the client's own sense of self, that he or she will then be dependent upon you and the cliché is 'You have not taught them how to fish, you have merely given them a fish to eat'. If you withold advice then somehow they will generate solutions for themselves. On the contrary, without receiving advice they may never see the light. What I have found in my practice is that when I give advice, clients come to believe that they arrived at the conclusions without input from me. I may say, 'I would advise you to discuss the situation with your brother because you will feel very guilty in the long run if you don't do that. This is my advice.' And the person may answer, 'No, I don't think I want to discuss it with my brother, I don't think it will work', so we let it go. Two or three weeks later, the person comes into therapy and says, 'You know what I've decided? I have decided I want to have a discussion with my brother. If I don't I will probably end up feeling guilty and so I have made up my mind to go ahead and we are going to meet on Friday night and discuss the matter.' They have now owned it; I have planted the seed and it grew over time although initially the person rejected it out of hand. So advice-giving, I think, is a very important part of therapy and I will often be fairly free with my advice always phrasing it, 'This is the way I see it, this is my subjective opinion'. The advice is not given in a dictatorial sense. I might parenthetically say that I feel that our state of knowledge is such that it is important for us to be humble and to state things tentatively. 'This is my subjective opinion, this is how I see it, according to my perceptions, so-and-so seems to be the case.' You see there's a difference between saying 'I think it would be a good idea if you chatted to your brother' and 'You must do that'. Let's avoid being presumptuous, or arrogant. So advice-giving is not instruction-giving; it's sharing an impression, a suggestion, a feeling and letting the person run with it and make a decision.

Windy Dryden: One of the phrases you mentioned earlier was 'It depends', and I think you would be the first to caution against changing an absolute don't into an absolute do. Therefore, when would you not give a client advice?

Arnold Lazarus: A very good point. Every do and don't can have its exceptions. At times I have given advice, and I have found that the person had distorted what I had said. For example I might have said, 'I think it would be a good idea if you thought of changing jobs in the near future'. And the person comes back and says, 'Last time you told me that I should go and have it out with my boss and really confront him'. These distortions need to be guarded against. When I discover that I am dealing with the kind of person who distorts and twists suggestions that I make, I become wary. When I make a recommendation, I ask the person to repeat back to me what I have just said. At other times, I question the person and say, 'What do you think might be a good way to proceed?' and let them put forth a *modus operandi*. So there is one example of when I modify advice-giving or decide not to give advice.

Windy Dryden: Are there any other circumstances?

Arnold Lazarus: Yes. Some clients approach you with a plan that they want to bounce off somebody without being told what you think, how you view it, or what they should do. They are really not interested in that, but want to hear themselves talk to somebody, and then go ahead and do what they want to do, and unless there are good reasons for them to act differently, you might simply listen and say, 'What you have told me is very interesting', and avoid any kind of advice-giving or suggestions.

Windy Dryden: Let's go on to your next erroneous don't.

Arnold Lazarus: The next unfortunate don't is *'Don't self-disclose'*. I have been told that it is very important for the therapist to be an enigma, to be detached, somewhat impersonal and impartial and if you self-disclose you destroy the anonymity, you become too real. The person can no longer see in you what he or she wants to see in you, because you have disabused them, by giving them the truth. Selective self-disclosure can be very helpful, and often by saying to somebody 'I have been there' or 'I have felt that' or 'Let me tell you what I do when I feel depressed or if I get anxious', this can be extremely humanising and helpful to many people. Many have appreciated it greatly. The fact that the therapist is not playing the role of a god pretending to be perfect, but is willing to share shortcomings, limitations, fears and doubts that he or she has, will often break down barriers and enhance the development of trust. But let me emphasise that it can backfire with some people who wish to see the therapist as a model of complete adjustment. In my experience, such clients are in the minority. So selective self-disclosure can be very useful.

Windy Dryden: Distinctions have been made in the literature between coping self-disclosure and mastery self-disclosure. What you seem to be advocating is coping self-disclosure, where a therapist says 'Well, I have experienced similar difficulties to you in the past and this is how I personally overcame them', rather than mastery self-disclosure where a therapist says 'I have never had such a problem, because I have always believed this or I have always done that'.

Arnold Lazarus: And it's also fine to say, 'I am still struggling with some of those myself, I haven't entirely resolved them'. Now as already mentioned, the trouble with giving mastery disclosures is that they imply that the therapist is some impeccable, immaculate being who is totally out of orbit, with whom the client cannot identify, and that's rather unfortunate.

Perhaps I ought to add a few don'ts to the two I started out with: 'Don't boast and brag about how wonderful you are, and don't blow your own horn too loudly'. It certainly is useful at times, I might add, to build the placebo effect by mentioning some of one's credentials and training, but not by bragging or boasting. Mastery is not a good way to get people to make changes because they get discouraged, because it implies that perfect solutions exist, whereas in fact we struggle along, but some of us muddle through life better than others. If one can give this anti-perfectionistic aura of people struggling along and coping it's far more realistic than a picture of total mastery.

Windy Dryden: Now again adopting the principle of 'It depends', when might you not self-disclose to a client?

Arnold Lazarus: When clients are just not interested. I don't self-disclose when after revealing something about myself, it does not prove helpful, the person does not use this in the way I intended, or when he or she is quite disinterested. Also I would not self-disclose if I have evidence that the person may tend to use it against me, or will undermine the therapy. If I say, 'I am still struggling with specific issues in my own marriage', and the person comes back to the next session and begins to nail me, and proceeds to say that I need therapy myself because I am just as badly off as he or she is, I would make a mental note not to use self-disclosure that displays my own shortcomings to this person. Those I think are the main occasions when I would eschew that sort of intervention.

Windy Dryden: OK, let's have a look at the next fallacious don't on your list.

Arnold Lazarus: The next don't is a big one, *'Don't socialise'*, in fact it was *'Never socialise with clients'*. 'Boundary' was a very big word that some of my supervisors employed, implying that if you went beyond the confines of the consulting room, you would undermine your power and your efficacy.

The idea that you might in fact accept a dinner invitation to a client's home, the fact that you might invite a client to join you at a movie, was unthinkable and strongly proscribed. There are many therapists who operate under these very rigid rules. I have sometimes found that I have gained information at a dinner party, on a tennis court or while taking a walk with a client, that would never have come out in my consulting room. I am just sorry that I don't have the opportunity to spend more time observing my clients in their natural habitat as it were. It's a little artificial just seeing them within the confines of four walls. But I don't want the reader to get the wrong impression. I do *not* spend a lot of time socialising with my clients; this is something that has been very selective. I would say that out of thousands of clients I have treated, I may have socialised with a few dozen, which is not a very high percentage. When I have socialised, it's been because I have sensed that this would be advantageous and that there was no *a priori* reason not to do so.

Windy Dryden: What therapeutic reasons have you had for socialising with your clients?

Arnold Lazarus: I sensed for example with one man, that he believed that I considered myself superior to him, and that if push came to shove, I would not want to be in his company, outside of my office. As long as he was paying me money, I would put up with him. This was not verbalised, but seemed to come through in some subtle innuendoes. During a session he asked if my wife and I would like to come to his house for dinner, and he gave me a particular date. I immediately thanked him and accepted the invitation. I could see that he was very pleased that I hadn't given him the professional brush-off. And indeed going to his home turned the therapy around and it gave him a feeling of acceptance that was far greater than I could give him in a professional role. Later when I reciprocated and invited this man and his wife to our home for dinner, with some of our mutual friends, this meant a great deal to him. And he said, as therapy progressed, this was pivotal in his experience.

Similarly a woman who was in therapy with me because of certain feelings of inferiority nevertheless described herself as a good tennis player. I called her up one evening and explained that my wife and I played tennis with another couple, but the wife of the other man was unable to come, and asked her if she would fill in. This meant a tremendous amount to her, and these kinds of gestures facilitated what we were doing and accomplishing in therapy. Now again, I knew my customer, I didn't just randomly do this, but from what had happened in the therapy, I deduced that this would be positive. I have at times been wrong.

Windy Dryden: Let's talk about some of those times. What were the factors that led you to conclude that you were wrong?

Arnold Lazarus: Well, talking about tennis, on another occasion with a different person, when I had invited her to play tennis, she thought I was making an overture, and she thought that this was my way of trying to seduce her. In her mind, asking her to play tennis meant something else and that we would eventually end up in bed. This emerged in the session after I called her; she had declined to come to tennis and I noticed that she was different in that session, though I was pleased that she brought it up. She could have been scared right out of therapy. After mentioning these thoughts, I expressed my gratitude to her for sharing them, and assured her that this was not my agenda.

Windy Dryden: As most instances of sex between therapists and clients occur between male therapists and female clients should male therapists be more circumspect, particularly with their female clients, about extending the boundaries of therapy into the area of socialising?

Arnold Lazarus: You have to be careful that you don't play into certain fantasies. One of my students is a young, extremely attractive male, and I caution him, more so than I would your average-looking individual, to beware of the fantasies that he can engender with gay men and with heterosexual female clients. Such a man inviting clients to have dinner with him, play tennis with him or go to a movie with him, would carry a far greater risk than would be true of less good-looking clinicians. I think people have to know their reinforcement value and limitations and operate within those.

Windy Dryden: Let's go back to the man who said that socialising with you was a pivotal point in his therapy. What if he wanted to develop the friendship further and you didn't?

Arnold Lazarus: Yes, it could become a problem, but no more of a problem than somebody in therapy who decides that you are fantastic and wants to continue seeing you, while you want to terminate the therapy because you consider that you have done all you can for this person. It's a little bit more touchy outside the consulting room but again I would be inclined to be frank and to say to this person that in fact my social calendar is very full and although we could be good, casual friends, the demands of my job, family, writing, research, travels, lectures, would make another continuous ongoing social interaction very difficult. So I would keep the social interaction on an occasional basis. I don't think the person would come away devastated or crushed, but it would pose a dilemma. The opposite has happened, a couple of times, where lasting friendships did develop after therapy ended. But I have been rather cautious in these matters and that is why I have not fallen into the awkward situation you posed earlier.

Windy Dryden: When would you definitely not extend the relationship outside of the boundaries of therapy?

Arnold Lazarus: If I sensed that there were ulterior motives and if I felt that the kind of unhappy ending that you alluded to was likely to occur. It is not difficult to size most people up and deduce that they will escalate matters, seek more and more reassurance, and end up feeling rejected. In these cases you can hide behind the shibboleth that it is against the ethical rules to socialise, so the person doesn't feel so rejected.

I also would not socialise if I thought that there was some form of exploitation. Now this did happen on one occasion when I read cues incorrectly. This very wealthy man, who was in therapy with me for some obsessive–compulsive problems, extended a dinner invitation and I accepted. Subsequently I realised that what had happened was that he had invited a number of people and had expected me to be the entertainer to enhance his social image. He wanted to display me like a trophy, that his friend was a well-known psychologist, a raconteur and the life-and-soul of the party (a mutual acquaintance had so characterised me). I was in rather a pensive mood that night and preferred to take a back seat and observe and discuss issues with one or two people in a quiet fashion. He came to the next session extremely annoyed with me for having let him down. In no uncertain terms he told me what a social dud I was. So you see by accepting his social invitation I had made an error. Sometimes, however, those mistakes can be brought back into the therapy and used to the advantage of the client.

Windy Dryden: In terms of countertransference, before extending the boundaries of therapy do you examine your own motives?

Arnold Lazarus: Yes, I think that what some call countertransference is important in this regard. Why do I do what I am doing? We need to examine what impact our personalities are having on others and we need to examine why we ourselves develop certain feelings or reactions to our clients. There have been occasions, however, when there has not been time to examine the countertransference. Somebody comes up with a suggestion, 'Why don't we take a walk instead of sitting in the office?', and you instantly see that this is some kind of test. To pass the test you must agree instantly. You haven't had a chance to examine your own feelings and motivations; you are responding to the immediacy of the request, and hope that you read the signals correctly.

Windy Dryden: When you have had the opportunity to examine your own motives, have you decided that your motives weren't as 'kosher', as they should be, with the result that you decided not to extend the boundaries?

Arnold Lazarus: One case that comes to mind was when I was treating a publisher and he had extended an invitation for me to come to a party and I wanted very much to accept. But I had the time to think about why I was so eager and soon saw that it was because it would have given me a chance to meet some influential people who could have furthered what I was doing, as far as certain writings were concerned. I felt to myself that this was an unfair exploitation, and that it would also, in a certain sense, make me beholden to this man and weaken what was happening in our therapy. Here was a man of enormous power who had no power over me up to that point. I was purely his therapist and I declined because I thought that would undermine what we were trying to do. So this was one fairly recent case in point.

Windy Dryden: Let's have a look at your next don't.

Arnold Lazarus: The next unfortunate don't is *'Don't accept gifts from clients'*. I was on a panel with a psychoanalyst some years back in Arizona; a member of the audience had asked about the accepting of gifts and he had said that he never would accept gifts. What he would do, would be to interpret what was happening: he would honour the moment, but he would not accept the gift. Instead he would make the person aware of his or her motivations, whatever they might be. And humorously I said surely it depends on the gift. With tongue in cheek I said if I was being offered a cheap tie I too would handle it in that way, I would not accept it. I would examine the motivation (by the way, we were addressing an audience of over 1000 people). I went on to say that if the person was offering me a Mercedes Benz I would accept it graciously and drive away in it. When the laughter died down, I took a more serious position and said, 'It depends'. When would and wouldn't one accept gifts? There are some people who you know very well who would come with gifts in the hope of owning you or feeding into some of their paternal or maternal fantasies and it's not a good idea to go ahead and play into this. You may want to point out to them what you think is happening. But with most people who offer a little gift like a tie at Christmas time, a nice pair of socks, a tee shirt or something they might have picked up on vacation, there's no need to suspect ulterior motives. It's such an insult not to graciously say, 'Thank you very much, I appreciate that; how nice of you to think of me on your vacation. I am really touched. I look forward to wearing this'. End of story without any interpretation. But I had one client who started plying me with many small gifts and immediately we had to stop this, for obvious reasons, and examine what was happening. I had another client whom I knew to be at the time a compulsive shop-lifter who offered me the most magnificent sweater I have seen in years. I asked if she had paid for it. And she said, 'I cannot tell a lie, I stole it'. I said, 'Well, as much as it hurts me, I cannot accept stolen goods, but thank you for the thought: you and I have got to try and work on your moral hierarchy'.

Windy Dryden: You joked that you would accept a valuable gift, and turn down a less valuable one, but in reality would you accept a gift that you considered was more than a token of appreciation?

Arnold Lazarus: No, the truth is, if somebody offers a gift that is more than, as you say, a token, I think it would be a mistake to accept it, because I think that then one is beholden; it smacks of bribery and it would feel like a power play. Also there are some very interesting ethical issues that have been spelt out by the American Psychological Association. Somebody who is a shareholder of vast corporations offers to give the therapist a gift of 1000 shares which could be worth 10 000 dollars in a year or two. It would be a big mistake to accept the offer. It runs counter to the ethics of the American Psychological Association. There are some definite rules and regulations to follow in this regard.

Windy Dryden: Have you ever given gifts to clients?

Arnold Lazarus: You know, I am sure I have, although offhand I cannot recollect any. I often give books to clients, if that can be said to be giving gifts. I give many of my self-help books to clients hoping that this will facilitate therapy.

Windy Dryden: You don't charge them for the books?

Arnold Lazarus: Right, I don't charge them. Suppose a client said to me he had to go to a very important dinner and needed to borrow a tie, I'm sure I'd let him borrow or keep one of my ties. I could see myself doing that, but offhand I don't know if I have actually given gifts other than books.

Windy Dryden: Have you ever sent a client a Christmas or birthday card, which is in a sense a gift?

Arnold Lazarus: Yes, I have done that on occasion. I have this one client who was very disturbed, a young woman who had been brutally raped by her mother's brother when she was 9, and whose father had died shortly before that, and who regarded me at the end of therapy as her adopted father, sent me cards on Father's day and on my birthday and, although I have not seen her in therapy now for a good four or five years, I have noted her birthday in my diary and I send her a birthday card, and I know it means a lot to her, and it is always signed YAD, which means 'Your adopted dad'.

Windy Dryden: 'Let's have a look at the next don't on your list.

Arnold Lazarus: The next one is *'Don't challenge or confront patients'*.

Windy Dryden: Now of course in some therapies like rational–emotive therapy or gestalt therapy that isn't a don't. So could we consider in what way it was a don't as part of your training?

Arnold Lazarus: It was part of my training because initially I was taught by psychodynamic and Freudian practitioners to avoid any kind of confrontation, and to be very sparse even with any interpretations. However, there is something to be said against challenging or confronting, when it is done without class. I have seen it carried out in a brash and unfortunate manner, and the person can emerge feeling attacked and hurt. The distinction that is so often drawn between challenging a person's behaviour versus challenging the person is important here. When you challenge a person's behaviour and accept the person, he or she may well feel unconditional regard as a human being, but when you challenge the person as a whole, he or she may well feel put down by you. So challenging and confronting must be done with finesse, with grace, or it can backfire. But I don't think we have to dwell too much on that, because there are many schools of thought today that don't, even for a moment, subscribe to this particular don't.

Windy Dryden: So let's move on to your next unfortunate don't.

Arnold Lazarus: The next don't I want to mention is somewhat tied into the one about not accepting gifts, and it's *'Don't accept favours'*. A client says something like, 'I will look up this reference for you and pop it in the mail' or 'Why don't I give you a ride to pick up your car at the service station: it is on my way'. My teachers would recommend against accepting favours. Even worse would be for the therapist to ask for a favour: 'I wonder if you would do me a favour, and mail this letter for me, if you pass a mail box on the way home'. I was told in my training days you must never do that. Now there is a fine dividing line here, of course, between accepting small favours and exploiting certain patients. Obviously I am against exploitation. There are those who would argue that asking somebody to mail a letter is exploitation. I think that's silly. If psychotherapy is practised under the guise of some stylised professionalism, it becomes arid, dry, sterile and inhuman. But if we see therapy as involving human beings working together with a view to being helpful, solving problems and pooling resources, then there is more fluidity and freedom. Would I hesitate to say to a colleague, be a pal and mail this letter for me? No. Why would I then hesitate with a client? It's different, if the person says no, they are not going anywhere near a mail box, but they will drive four miles out of their way in the snow to mail this letter for me: that would be exploitation. So I say that part of being a human therapist is you can accept small favours and often make minor requests.

Windy Dryden: Again have there been times when you have regretted doing so, when it has turned out to be a mistake?

Arnold Lazarus: Yes. One of the problems about working the way I do is that I sometimes have regrets and there are times when I am well aware that Freudians and Rogerians never get into this kind of hot water.

Windy Dryden: Partly because it seems as though you are prepared to take more risks?

Arnold Lazarus: That's correct. I have been lucky that most of them have paid off, they have paid dividends, but there have been instances when I have regretted it. Some people can easily feel abused or taken advantage of. A client might say, 'You have a nerve asking me to drop a package off with my next-door neighbour. I am not a delivery boy. You can deliver it yourself.' This is an actual quote. What had happened in the session was the person had mentioned that he lived next door to certain people who were expecting a package from me, they were next-door neighbours. This had come out for-tuitously, and I said, 'How funny, I have a package I am about to mail to them', and the client said, he would be glad to drop it off, since it's right next door. He actually made the offer. When I took him up on it and said that would be very kind of him, it would certainly speed things up, later, in the session the client changed his mind and accused me of having a darn nerve.

Windy Dryden: How did you respond?

Arnold Lazarus: I responded by saying that the offer appeared to be a genuine offer, that it was perhaps a test which I failed. If I had passed the test I would have insisted on going to the Post Office myself. I also en-quired whether he had changed his mind because he did not want his neighbours to find out that he was undergoing therapy. The client denied the latter but confirmed the former. So I pointed out that because he had made an offer that he wanted me to refuse, he was not being authentic with me. I said something like, 'I believed you, when you said it was no trouble, and accepted your kindness. On the other hand, does this mean that this is how you are with other people as well, is this something you do? Do you perhaps set up other people in this fashion by tricking them in this way? You tricked me into accepting what I thought was a simple kind offer.' So I was able to get therapeutic mileage out of it.

Windy Dryden: That leads us on to another viewpoint which I have heard stated quite frequently, namely that the way the client interacts with his or her therapist is somehow prototypical of the way that he or she reacts to other people in his or her social world. Does this notion have much validity or is it a sacred cow?

Arnold Lazarus: I regard it as a sacred cow and think that it has to be checked out. In the foregoing example, we had a case in which I was asking, whether a prototypical pattern had emerged. One might ask, 'Is this person-specific or do you set up others similarly?' or 'Is this the only time this has happened in your life?', 'Is this the first time you have done such a thing?' or 'Is this something you do with most other people?'. It turned out that in the foregoing case this was something he did frequently and that it was prototypical. But it doesn't have to be a general pattern. Of course we all have a fairly consistent way of responding when we feel cheated, or angry, or misunderstood, and so forth.

Clients who view you as a parent figure may be inclined to treat you or relate to you as they do their parents. If they regard you as a policeman or an authority figure, then maybe they will relate to you as they would relate to a policeman or other figures. But they won't relate to you as they do to their friends or their siblings, because you are perceived in a different light. So you have to check the person's specific perceptions, feelings and apperceptions; it's of course not unreasonable to assume that people have a limited repertoire and the way they respond in the office to a given situation might very well be the same way that they would respond in a different setting. I remember a situation in which a student therapist was working under my supervision, and he made a remark that his client regarded as an ethnic slur. The client became enraged, and bellowed at the therapist. Now the question here was, is this how he would have responded to most people, or was there something about the student-therapist that was annoying him in particular? This needs to be checked out instead of automatically calling it 'negative transference'. It turned out that this man's volatile temper was one of his major problems. The way he blew up at the therapist was put to good effect in the therapy by showing this man that it is preferable to respond assertively by simply saying, 'Gee I feel that's an ethnic slur, that's a put-down, I find that a very distressing expression that you have used', and thus to deal with it in a civilised assertive fashion.

Windy Dryden: As we are discussing this issue, what is your position on the issue of transference in multimodal therapy?

Arnold Lazarus: Transference has been written about extensively by psychoanalytic practitioners and is a vast and complex subject. Let's refer to a few basic observations. It is not difficult to see or understand that you can transfer your affections from one person to another, negatively and positively, that somebody may meet you as a therapist and feel very good about you, because perhaps you remind them of someone who was kind to them when they were little. A woman came and told me that she was very nervous about her session, but the moment she saw me she was at ease because I reminded her very much of her father, with whom she had a good relationship. You see that's an example of so-called transference: 'He reminds me of my father; my father was good, so he will be good.' If the father had been nasty, this could have contaminated our relationship and she could have developed a negative transference. I think there's validity in those straightforward issues. We have all had the experience of disliking somebody intensely even though we don't know him or her, and if asked why, we would probably have to delve into our memories and dig up the fact that this person reminds us, looks like, acts like, moves like, somebody we have good reason to dislike from our past experiences. This is what learning theorists call stimulus generalisation and response generalisation. Working with a positive transference which, to my mind, translates into rapport, a good working relationship, a healthy liaison, tends to facilitate the goals of most therapists. Taking transference beyond that delimited meaning, as many theorists have done, I think just muddies the waters. Once we start talking about repressed, unconscious, conflictual childhood memories or reliving deeply held infantile desires, we enter the quagmire of psychoanalytic speculations.

Windy Dryden: Many theoreticians and practitioners regard the relationship between the therapist and the client as the prime vehicle for change. True or sacred cow?

Arnold Lazarus: The relationship is the context that allows change to occur and is sometimes necessary and sufficient; often times it is necessary but insufficient. If you have a patient, who has a bipolar disorder and is in a manic phase, it matters little how good the relationship is, the chances are that this person will continue to suffer until treated with the right medication, which is lithium.

Windy Dryden: But if you have a good relationship with such clients, this may encourage them to take their medication.

Arnold Lazarus: Correct, but you cannot ascribe the change to the relationship. The relationship, will foster the technique. If you have a good relationship, you might be able to encourage phobic patients to expose themselves to their feared situations thereby mitigating the phobias, you might encourage obsessives or compulsives to stop their rituals thereby producing an attenuation of their habit patterns, you may be able to persuade the unassertive person to take risks, so yes, the relationship is necessary but insufficient. But again I have to say that there are so many conditions where the most empathic, wonderful, understanding relationship will not produce change of any significance, unless within that context of a good relationship the proper techniques are correctly applied.

Chapter 7
Counselling on TV
An Interview with John Cobb

John Cobb qualified as a medical doctor in 1966. As a houseman he drew comment from his consultants that his social and personal histories were as long if not longer than his description of the strictly medical history and physical examination. 'Really Cobb!' one professor of paediatrics commented, 'Only a line or two is needed about the general background.'

Impressed with the importance of pursuing a career as a 'proper doctor', he stayed with hospital medicine for 3 years, working in teaching hospitals gaining knowledge of a plethora of rare syndromes and qualifying as a Member of the Royal College of Physicians.

At this point, motivated as much by a decision to travel as by increasing frustration with the mechanistic approach of academic medicine, he took a job as a medical officer in Uganda. Two years in Africa, at the time General Amin took over power, could not but broaden his horizons. An interest in the way the body works was developed into a fascination with the way people live, and why they behave the way they do.

On return to the UK, a year in general practice impressed him with the importance of achieving as much as possible within a brief meeting, 10 minutes being the maximum that could be allowed per patient in a busy clinic.

Inevitably he then gravitated towards the study of psychiatry. Perhaps the seeds of this interest had been sown when reading William Sargeant's book *Battle for the Mind* at the age of 16. Though Sargeant's 'magic bullet' approach by now seemed dated, a period of 6 years' study and research at the Maudsley Hospital and Institute of Psychiatry, confirmed his conviction that psychiatry was the career he wanted to follow.

Though he considers himself to be first and foremost a medical doctor, John Cobb was fortunate while at the Maudsley to work for a consultant who is a world leader in behaviour therapy (Professor Isaac Marks), an influential Kleinian psychoanalyst (Dr John Steiner) and a senior consultant in group analytic work (Dr Malcolm Pines). Psychological methods of treatment became a special interest and for 7 years he worked as Senior Lecturer in Psychotherapy and Consultant Psychiatrist at St George's Hospital. While in this post Dr Cobb developed an interest in cognitive therapy, which proved to be a fruitful theoretical and practical framework for using an electic psychological approach to the management of patients. He was in charge of a special unit for the treatment of obsessional and anxiety-related disorders. Through this unit came his first contract with television, when Steven Rose of the BBC (*QED* programme) filmed the progress of a lady with disabling obsessional rituals from assessment to the end of treatment (fortunately successful!).

Teaching was an important part of this job, and Dr Cobb worked closely with an imaginative family therapist (Dr Stuart Lieberman). Together they developed an interview skills training course which they called 'The Grammar of Psychotherapy' and which was taught to a wide range of medical and paramedical personnel.

Increasing frustration with the National Health Service led John Cobb to move into private practice 7 years ago. A link with academic psychiatry was preserved through a senior clinical tutor attachment at the Maudsley Hospital, where, together with Dr Stirling Mooray and Ruth Williams, he set up the first training course in the UK in cognitive psychotherapy.

He now has his own practice in Knightsbridge and holds a contract with The Priory Hospital in Roehampton.

Windy Dryden: I would like to focus this interview on your experiences of working as a counsellor on the late night television counselling programme entitled *A Problem Aired*. Perhaps you could start off by briefly describing it and saying a little bit about how you became involved in it.

John Cobb: I got involved right at the start. One of the producers from Thames Television came to see me and asked what I thought about the idea of seeing somebody who I hadn't met beforehand and talking to them for 10–20 minutes on television. After that I didn't hear from them for about a year, until I received a phone call from Liz Neeson, a producer, who had taken over and developed the idea. I was quite short with her, actually, because I had already given an hour of my time and got nothing back. However, Liz and I met over lunch and talked it through, and from that discussion the programme started. So it was basically their idea, but I put in a few points, such as the condition that the interviews shouldn't be broken up by adverts in the middle. I thought that was most important. We actually started off by doing two 10-minute interviews.

Windy Dryden: On the same programme?

John Cobb: Yes. But now we do one that lasts for about 20 minutes. I had all sorts of doubts about it to start with, as you can imagine.

Windy Dryden: What were you doubtful about?

John Cobb: Well, first of all we all knew this was a risk. Who would be watching at 1 a.m., for example? We also thought we might get a very odd group of people: histrionic, in search of publicity, presenting pseudo problems; I also thought that it would be difficult to do much in 20 minutes, and even more so in 10 minutes. Having said that, I have done quite a lot of work on what you can achieve in a GP interview, which is normally about 7 minutes, and I have run workshops on a 7-minute interview; people are usually surprised to find how much you can get out of a few minutes if you set about it the right way. The other big doubt I had was that the television producers would see the programme primarily as show business rather than anything educational or therapeutic.

Windy Dryden: So your doubts focused on what kind of clients you would get and on whether the TV people would try to make it more showbiz.

John Cobb: That's right, I was worried that they would go for the more dramatic or bizarre problems, the ones that would get people titillated.

Windy Dryden: Were either of your doubts confirmed in that respect?

John Cobb: Neither of them was. One of the people who subsequently became involved in the series, Jenny Cozens, did a psychological survey, and contacted the first 40 programme guests, who had various psychological profiles, and showed that their problems were identical to those presented by people who turn up for psychiatric help: anxiety, depression, relationship problems, abuse of alcohol, anorexia, and one or two more serious psychiatric problems that we filtered out. So the problems were very typical and the people came from all walks of life.

Windy Dryden: What were your criteria for selection?

John Cobb: There is an advert on the programme that gives a number to ring or an address to write to. People who want to know more about counselling are then sent a booklet with a number of local counselling addresses and information about counselling generally. If they decide they want to appear on the programme they are seen by one of the researchers, who are university graduates without any special training in counselling, but are by and large good at talking to people, eliciting information and writing down what people say, and who carry out a preliminary selection. This entails contacting relatives, talking to the person on the phone, getting them to come to the studio, talking to them in depth for an hour or two, and then producing a protocol. They are adept at spotting hidden agendas. I see five or six protocols for each programme then sit down with the producer and researcher, and we go through them together and make the final choice.

Windy Dryden: What are you looking for at that point?

John Cobb: I am looking for an identifiable, focused problem, and for somebody who is likely to be able to communicate in front of the cameras. Intelligence hasn't been an issue, but somebody who is very inarticulate or tends to be monosyllabic and difficult to engage wouldn't be suitable for the programme.

Windy Dryden: Is that because you feel that you won't get anywhere or that it won't make good television?

John Cobb: Both, I think. I see it as an educational endeavour, as much as a therapeutic endeavour. I am not really there to treat one individual: I am there to show people what one type of psychotherapeutic approach is like and what it can achieve. For many people this is not an end in itself, it's the first step towards doing more. We are also looking for a wide range of people, so if we had three female clients we would be looking for a male, if we had three young people we would be looking for somebody older, and so on. Of course we are looking for people with different problems: if we had three people with anxieties, for instance, we would be looking for someone with a different problem.

Windy Dryden: So to sum up you are looking for a clear focus that you can work with in the time available, for somebody who is likely to be able to communicate, and for diversity with respect to gender, age and the nature of the problem.

John Cobb: That's right. We exclude people who are actively pscychotic, people who turn up drunk or drugged, and also those who we sense are looking for publicity.

We have had approaches from one or two people, for instance, who have been on various quiz shows and seem to make a hobby out of appearing on television. There are also people who have particular axes to grind and may want to try and make a point on television. Obviously we do not want to get involved in that. Having said that, it doesn't matter if people are young or old, intelligent, university-educated or unsophisticated and have left school at 15. We certainly see people from all walks of life.

Windy Dryden: When do you first meet the client?

John Cobb: I don't meet them until just a few minutes before we go on the set, and even then I will just say hello, shake their hand, ask them what they would like me to call them when we meet and if there is anything they really don't want to talk about. I deliberately don't take it further than that, because I think it would detract from the freshness of our first interaction, which we want to capture on camera.

Windy Dryden: Do you use their real names?

John Cobb: Yes, but only their first names. We have never had anybody who did not want to be called by his or her real name.

Windy Dryden: How much information do you have prior to that?

John Cobb: Well, I have quite a lot of information, based on the interview that the researcher carried out. They take better histories than a lot of medical students, or even than a lot of psychiatrists, because they write as a novelist might write, with very good descriptions of things they noticed as well as a verbatim report of what was said.

They cover both the past and the present problems, but from a totally non-medical, even non-psychotherapeutic, point of view. They are just good honest descriptions. Sometimes we have information from husband or wife, mother or father, or a 'referee', who is just somebody we can talk to about the individual.

Windy Dryden: What is the purpose of that?

John Cobb: Well, one reason is to get some idea about the authenticity of the person's story. Another reason why we contact the relatives, in particular, is to make sure that they know what is going to happen and are in favour of it. If a spouse or a parent were to be strongly against the person appearing on TV, we would have serious doubts about going ahead. There is also a therapeutic reason, which is that it may be constructive for the person to discuss his or her problem with members of their family, perhaps for the first time, before coming on television.

Windy Dryden: You have mentioned in passing that your major aim is educational. What about your other aims for this particular programme.

John Cobb: One of the aims is to get people who feel, for instance, that they can't cope, that life is awful and everything is going wrong, to focus on one or two issues, and then look at why those particular issues might be difficult for them. Very often it is a question of reframing. For example, a patient may seem to be bogged down and unable to sustain relationships, but the problem may in fact be related to unresolved grief over the death a few years before of someone important, for example. In such cases I would try to help the patient to look at his or her difficulties from a different point of view. And a lot of people who have been on the programme do say, either during the interview or afterwards, that their perspective on the problem has changed. I try to promote a psychological, intrapsychic angle on the problem, to encourage people to see that problems stem from their attitudes and outlook and the way they react to the world. The reason, for example, why a woman seems to be let down time and again by men may be to do with her attitude towards men.

Windy Dryden: Is this shift to a different perspective something that people can use later?

John Cobb: Yes, or there and then. There was a 44-year-old woman who had been paralysed by a stroke, as a result of which she had become very depressed and had undergone a change of personality. She clearly believed that all that she had to give was her ability to look after the house, iron the shirts and so on. As she couldn't do that any more she felt she was useless.

She had never actually checked this out with her husband, but she did check it out with him in front of the camera, and he said that of course she wasn't useless, that there were all sorts of reasons why she was important to himself and the family, apart from cleaning the floors and ironing the shirts. And that in itself would be looking at things from a different point of view.

Windy Dryden: How does the medium of television affect your normal therapeutic style?

John Cobb: This framework actually suits me rather well, because I am an active therapist, I am fairly confrontational, and I work on a short-term basis. By short term I normally mean 6–10 hours rather than 20 minutes. But even in a first session with someone in my practice I am not just getting information, I am encouraging people to reconsider the way they look at things, the way they handle information, the way they see the world and so on. So my cognitive–behavioural orientation makes it much easier for me to work within the framework of the programme. It would be harder for a person-centred counsellor who would tend to be reflective and spend a lot of time patiently building up a relationship. I tend to build up a relationship by being active and by engaging people fairly briskly; on the other hand, I normally do an assessment in an hour and a half, so there is certainly a time difference.

Windy Dryden: Although, as you said earlier, quite a bit of that is done for you anyway.

John Cobb: That's right, a lot of the information has been gathered. In my regular practice, about an hour of my initial interview would be spent getting information and half an hour discussing the information I have obtained. I think that is where my approach differs from the normal psychiatric assessment in which the psychiatrist may spend an hour taking a history but won't have the time to discuss it.

On the programme I tend to be more focused: I deliberately decide to pick one or possibly two, but certainly not more than two, issues which seem to me to be fairly central or to reflect characteristics of the person, and I concentrate on these. Whereas in a normal assessment I would leave it up to the individual to choose which issues to work on, on the programme I do the choosing for them.

Being directive entails cutting people off sometimes, and perhaps missing things as a result.

Windy Dryden: Do you feel constrained at all by the medium of television, in the sense of being aware of the cameras, for example, or of how you want to come across? Are there any inhibiting factors?

John Cobb: There certainly were to start with. I feel less constrained now, and if I see myself working on the video recording of one of these interviews I seem to be pretty much the same as when I am sitting down with a patient in my practice.

Windy Dryden: What were the constraints at the start?

John Cobb: I probably pre-scripted the interview. I rehearsed in my head how I wanted it to go, and attempted to stick to the script. Watching the video afterwards I could see myself going through my script and ignoring the cues that were coming from the patient. Now I think I am much more responsive to the patient.

Windy Dryden: What do you think the motivation was for the scripting effect?

John Cobb: I wanted to put on what I thought was a good performance, but that matters less to me now that I have done it for about two and a half years. Other people have done it and dropped out; I am one of the survivors. There must be something about what I do that matches what is wanted so I don't feel that I have to prove anything to anybody any more.

Windy Dryden: Is it that you've made your mark?

John Cobb: I must have done, yes. Having said this, I probably shan't be rehired for the next series, I don't know.

Windy Dryden: I wonder how much cognitive–behavioural work you think you can do in the time you have available to you.
   I watched, in preparation for this interview, four or five of the recent programmes, and it seemed to me that the cognitive–behavioural conceptualisation on each station is clearly there, but that it was difficult for you really to focus on the cognitive–behavioural factors within that time span. Would you agree on that?

John Cobb: I think it's latent. A lot of it is not really cognitive–behavioural at all. It is more of a general psychotherapeutic interchange than the application of a particular model. But I don't think that I am purely cognitive–behavioural in my clinical practice either. I was trained in it, have taught it and I can play the role of a cognitive–behaviour therapist when I am with students. However, if you were a patient sitting there, I don't think I would be particularly cognitive; I would be interested in what was going through your mind at a particular moment, in the way you saw the world and whether that was valid or invalid, but I would also be interested in your unconscious, dreams, childhood, the relationship you had with your father and so on.

Windy Dryden: So you don't feel constrained by a particular model, and it seems quite important for you to be yourself on that programme.

John Cobb: Very much so. I would say that I am much more myself now that I am not trying to be Aaron Beck or Albert Ellis or whoever. I once had a brilliant supervision from Malcolm Pines at a time when I was having problems running a group. He asked what the problem was, and I said I didn't feel myself in the group. He asked 'Who do you feel you are?'. I replied 'I feel I am trying to be you'. He said 'Well, you are not me'. That helped a lot.

Windy Dryden: You mentioned earlier that it might be therapeutic for the client to talk to his or her family or to someone close, perhaps for the first time, about the problem, and that it might lead to a discussion within the family or the relationship. What would you say were the other therapeutic factors present in the programme?

John Cobb: First there is the recognition of having a problem, and of wanting to do something about it so much that they are prepared to put themselves through what for many people is a great ordeal. Then there is the Guru effect. Whether I was any good or not, the Guru factor would inevitably arise from going to see 'the great man' on television. People have said that was important. Third is the public confession, or public statement: 'I have a problem. I actually accept now that I am an alcoholic, I have never really accepted it before.' 'I accept that my compulsive gambling is ruining my family life.' 'I accept that I have to change in the way I look at this or that.' Did you see the young lad who cried about his mother's suicide? He had never actually said that to anybody before. He has now said it to a quarter of a million viewers in London. All this is nothing new; there is a long history of public healing, of standing up and making a confession, except that now we do it on television instead of at a church hall or in a stadium. I think the actual content is probably of less importance than the process. However, the content may be more important later. Some people have said that at the time they felt much better and didn't know why. They then played the recording over three or four times and thought about what was said, or discussed it with their partner and that seemed to help.

Windy Dryden: Are they given the video-tape at the end?

John Cobb: No, but they can get one if they want; most of them have got videos at home. One example which comes to mind where replaying the tape was helpful concerned a woman in the early days of the programme who suffered from a prolonged grief reaction for a child of 18 months who died of acute uvulitis (inflammation of the uvula, a part of the throat) within 12 hours after admission to hospital. She was a pretty cool and sophisticated American woman, but when I asked something about her relationship and sex life with her husband she ducked it, and I didn't press it, because I never push for catharsis. She told me afterwards, at a follow-up programme, that when she watched the video with her family, they turned it off at that point and said to her, 'You ducked that one, didn't you Mum?', and they then talked about what the issue was about which proved to be extremely helpful. In addition some people even get practical help and support, such as job or relationship offers from the viewers.

Windy Dryden: Do you have any examples of that?

John Cobb: We had a woman who was an obsessional hoarder: her room was so cluttered up that she couldn't get into her bed and her daughter couldn't get into her room because the house was full of stuff. A fairly distant friend saw the programme, rang up and said, 'I am coming round tomorrow to help you clear the house up'.

Another therapeutic point is that having done something memorable by appearing on television, people seem to feel a moral responsibility not to let life be the same as before.

Windy Dryden: Somehow it's an irreversible step for them.

John Cobb: I think so. We did a longer programme for the BBC on obsessions, which was about a woman who had been treated in the health service for 6 weeks both as an inpatient and an outpatient. The whole process was filmed by the BBC at various points; they took 15 hours of film and then they edited it down for a *QED* programme. I hadn't known how she was going to do and when I first saw her there I was worried that she wouldn't do well because she did not have strong motivation. But in the event she did extraordinarily well. She told me, 'You see, I felt everybody was so nice to me, I couldn't let them down'. So she, in a sense, got well for the BBC and for the viewers. People who take part on the programme say that they go on because they want to help other people: 'I want other people to know that they're not alone, that they could get help with this problem'; they want to show other people that they can improve.

Windy Dryden: Do you have any remaining qualms about the programme?

John Cobb: Well, I have qualms about the people who volunteer to come on, and who have very real problems, but who, for one reason or another, we have to reject.

We always offer them some alternative, suggest they go to a counselling association or their GP. So they get some advice, but they're rather left hanging in the air. We always have people come up as a standby just in case the main person doesn't turn up; sometimes the standby doesn't get on, and he or she may or may not get onto the programme subsequently. Also, some people have said that things have become difficult for them because of what came out on television.

Windy Dryden: Does the programme go out live?

John Cobb: We do the programme after lunch, and it goes the same night.

Windy Dryden: Do people have an opportunity to say, 'Well, I have been through it but I don't want this to go out'?

John Cobb: It is not an option and nobody has ever done it. By that stage they have been carefully talked through possible repercussions by the researcher. We ask them to think through beforehand, rather carefully, what the effect might be: 'What will your boyfriend say when he finds out you're morbidly jealous?', for example. If a case of sheer nerves arises, the standby guest is always there to step in.

Windy Dryden: So your qualms centre on a concern about the people who want to come on the programme, particularly those who come up on stand-by, and are not subsequently offered help, and about a few people who've had regrets about coming on the programme.

John Cobb: Yes. Initially I was worried that the producers might mess about with the programme, start editing it and so on, but they haven't done that. It's unedited, and I think that's very important.

Windy Dryden: I would like to focus on what the response to the programme has been; first of all from the general public and secondly from the world of counselling and psychotherapy.

John Cobb: Well, we know that about a quarter of a million people watch it and the numbers have held up; in fact they have increased. The programme receives letters from those people who have identified with those who have appeared on the programme and who have been thereby helped. Others decide to go for counselling as a result of seeing programmes. So obviously people watch it, whatever that tells you. In terms of the public responding to me, when people have recognised me, the response has been by and large pleasant. There have been a number of press articles, relating not only to *A Problem Aired* but also to a number of other programmes which have followed in its wake and which are often very different from it. There is one where they have a huge studio audience that is asked to choose which side of the family is right. Some pretty bizarre programmes get broadcast which to me just look like show business.

Windy Dryden: Do you get a lot of fan mail?

John Cobb: Not a lot, but a steady supply, some of which is crazy and some very appreciative. We are attracting a particular audience, people who are up at half past twelve at night anyway. What interests me is what a wide range of people seems to be up at this time watching television.

In terms of the counselling world we had a feedback day about two years ago, when various counselling associations were invited – there were the Westminster Pastoral Foundation, Relate, the Samaritans, the Jewish Marriage Guidance Council, the Catholic Marriage Guidance Council, someone from the Tavistock, and so on – we showed four or five programmes and then there was a lot of discussion. I thought we would get a lot of critical feedback: people saying that this wasn't really psychotherapy, that we were giving the false impression that these problems could be sorted out in a few minutes, and so on. But in fact the majority of people thought that it was a good educational experience and wanted the programmes shown at an earlier time and networked across Britain. They commented that it did take some of the mystery and fear out of counselling and that it was a good start. And after all, that is all we are trying to do: we are not saying that this is an end in itself, just that it's a good idea to sit down and talk to someone about your problems. As a direct result of having seen the programme, people had been turning up at their organisations and quite a few of them are now actually using tapes of the programmes in teaching, I gather, as a basis for seminars; presumably there are things that are worth copying, and also it can be useful to discuss our mistakes. Some of the interviews don't work, quite clearly. On some occasions I think that the person and I are like two ships passing in the night, with no link at all and I wonder what went wrong. We haven't ever not shown an interview that we have taped; we show them all, so you see good and bad.

Windy Dryden: Warts and all.

John Cobb: Yes.

Windy Dryden: One development in the programme has been that you and the client have the opportunity at the end of the programme to view the session on video-tape and talk about the client's impressions of what they have seen. Has this been an important development?

John Cobb: Yes, it's like a T-group, really. We found that when the cameras were turned off we would suddenly relax and *then* there would be an important interchange about a whole lot of interesting stuff that we hadn't covered before; and when we moved to the green room to have a cup of tea or a glass of wine even more material would come out. So we thought about all sorts of ways in which we could get a 'green room discussion' to show in the programme, and we decided to try this feedback. It is something I do in clinical practice anyway: I tend to give people a tape to take away and tell them to listen to it so that we can discuss it the following week. This is designed to capture the person's reaction to the therapeutic situation. It also initially came out of the fact that the presenter, who was a sort of third party who had been listening in, used to come and sit down at the end and say 'Why did you do this?' and 'Why did you do that?' or 'How did you feel?' – a mini-supervision, if you like. We want to do something more than just the counselling session.

Windy Dryden: Was it an opportunity for reflection?

John Cobb: Yes, that's right.

Windy Dryden: Finally, what do you think is the future for this programme?

John Cobb: I am sure that there must always be room for improvement and development, although I am not quite sure in which way it is going to go; I am really rather happy with the format we have got at the moment. I would like to see longer sessions, but I know there are constraints; half an hour would be better than 20 minutes, but to get a half-hour slot without any advertising breaks is asking rather a lot; so I would rather have 20 minutes uninterrupted than half an hour with a commercial break in the middle. But apart from that I wouldn't want to see any radical changes made.

Chapter 8
The Scientist as a Person
An Interview with John Marzillier

John Marzillier is joint head of the Oxford Regional Training Course in Clinical Psychology and Consultant Clinical Psychologist to the Oxfordshire Health Authority. In his clinical role he works as an NHS psychotherapist both in general practice and in psychiatric settings. He has had a long-standing interest in integrative therapies and in particular the relationship between cognitive and dynamic therapies.

In 1969 John started his professional career at the Maudsley Hospital, initially as a trainee clinical psychologist and then, for a further five years, as a lecturer and researcher on the clinical course. This was when behaviour therapy was in its heyday and John was actively involved in the development of behavioural treatments. His doctoral research, which he completed at this time, took the form of a controlled evaluation of social skills training for psychiatrically disturbed patients. His main clinical interests lay in individual therapy although he also had experience of group treatments. He lectured and published widely in behaviour therapy. He was a founder member of the British Association for Behavioural Psychotherapy (BABP) and went on to become its Treasurer and then Chairman.

In 1975 he was appointed as a lecturer in the Department of Psychology, University of Birmingham where he remained until 1982. During this period he continued his interest in psychological therapies, developed his research into social skills training, and supervised the research of many postgraduate students. A long-standing interest in cognitive factors and their role in therapeutic change led him in particular towards cognitive–behavioural therapy. On moving to his present position in Oxford, John was able to train as a cognitive therapist in the school developed by A. T. Beck. However, he never felt at home with the excessive rationalism of this therapy. A dormant interest in analytic therapies was revived and, following some supervision in dynamic psychotherapy, John embarked on a part-time psychotherapy course based at the Warneford Hospital, Oxford. He graduated with distinction from the course in 1990.

John is married to Mary who works as a student counsellor at the University of Oxford. They have two adolescent children who are in the throes of their secondary education at their local state school. He is a parent governor of his children's school, a supporter of Oxford United football club (for his sins), an enthusiastic theatre-goer, a lover of wildlife, birds of prey in particular, and fundamentally a hedonist (although the super-ego tends to get in the way). A year's sabbatical from his post has shown him the value of many things non-psychological and the singular importance of maintaining a detached perspective on the apparently momentous, but often trivial, activities of the professional group of psychotherapists to which he belongs.

Windy Dryden: In this interview, John, I would like to explore with you your development as a clinical psychologist first from being a behaviour therapist, then to becoming a cognitive–behaviour therapist, and finally to the present day where you are exploring the interface between cognitive and dynamic therapies. So, perhaps, we can start by going back to the earlier point in your career and find out what it was about behaviour therapy that attracted you.

John Marzillier: I suppose one starting point would be when I left Oxford and decided I wanted to train to be a clinical psychologist. I applied to two courses, one of which was the Tavistock course and the other the Maudsley course. I got a place on both those courses and I eventually went to the Maudsley and trained there. I have often thought back and wondered, if I had taken the Tavistock course, would my life have been rather different? It's one of those unanswerable questions because obviously I am looking back at it from the perspective I am at now. I turned down the Tavistock because of their attitude to criticism of the psychoanalytic approach. This was put succinctly by one of the people who interviewed me, that you have to have faith, and I didn't know that I could have sufficient faith, at that time, in the analytic approach. I was more interested in the applied scientific area, which was new and throwing up some interesting ideas and practices. So that was a choice point.

But I had always been interested in dynamic and analytic approaches. The first psychologist I read was Jung, before I went to Oxford, and one interest I have always had in psychology was to discover more about myself and other people. So there are these two sides which I think are in me, and probably in everybody, a more creative and subjective side and a more objective, scientific side.

Windy Dryden: Right. So we might be tempted to speculate that if the Tavistock had indicated to you that they were interested in a scientific attitude, you may well have ended up there rather than at the Institute of Psychiatry.

John Marzillier: Yes, but that's speculation. But when I came to the Maudsley it was at a change point itself for clinical psychology, which is another significant factor, because most of my initial training did not equip me for the work I went on to do. Most of the academic input and the clinical training was geared towards an assessment role, particularly psychometric testing, whereas psychologists were then beginning to carry out a therapeutic role, in the form of behaviour therapy, and it was clear to me immediately that a therapeutic role was much more attractive than pure assessment. There was a change going on and there was much enthusiasm, eagerness and excitement about the new movement. Behaviour therapy was tackling problems which had been difficult for traditional approaches to handle. I remember working with Jack Rachman at the beginning of his work on obsessional disorders. I was a therapist on one of the early cases and I was enormously impressed by the practicality, the forcefulness and the commonsense nature of the approach. There was a willingness to go out and try and help people who had been discarded or who had proved difficult to help. There was also a respect given to individual clients and care taken to avoid broad inferences made about underlying psychopathology. So that's what carried me along in behaviour therapy, I guess. And there is another aspect, the fact that the therapeutic approach gave quite a lot of power to psychologists because here were psychological procedures which *supposedly* were developed from academic psychology. The link is very tenuous in fact, but the link was very much in the mind of the people at the time and it enabled psychologists to be therapists very quickly. I wanted that opportunity.

Windy Dryden: What happened to your interest in the dynamic therapies at that time?

John Marzillier: It really went into abeyance for quite a period. I did my PhD, which was in the area of evaluating social skills training, and I was involved in developments within behaviour therapy. I was a founder member of the British Association for Behavioural Psychotherapy (BABP) and eventually went on to become its Chairman. So by and large I put aside my interest in the dynamic approach, except in as much as I was always interested in extending behaviour therapy beyond the rather limited view that some people had of it. I knew, from my work with social anxiety, about the importance of relationships for people, although social skills training as a method of therapy is rather limited. My own research had failed to show that it was particularly effective for the people I tried it out on. I think that looking at social and relationship problems impinges on the dynamic approach, even though I didn't at that stage apply it to myself as a therapist. I still saw myself in the mode of someone who helps other people by applying knowledge, in other words, as an applied scientist.

Windy Dryden: In terms of your professional self-identity, though, at that time, were you happy to call yourself a behaviour therapist?

John Marzillier: Oh yes, I was and I did. I felt that you could encompass within behaviour therapy a lot of the developments which came to be known as cognitive–behaviour therapy. And then eventually, more recently, I moved into cognitive therapy. I wasn't very familiar with rational–emotive therapy, I'm afraid.

Windy Dryden: We can forgive you for that!

John Marzillier: I thought you might say that! I accepted behaviour therapy as a paradigm that I was working within and I saw it as a developing paradigm.

Windy Dryden: OK, so you were happy to call yourself a behaviour therapist, you saw it as a fairly broad model which could encompass various concepts which had perhaps been neglected by other behaviour therapists, but you could see a way of fitting it under the behavioural umbrella. At what point did you start to question that particular professional self-identity?

John Marzillier: That's difficult to know. I think it began almost from the very beginning and it became more salient, I suppose, when I started my interest in cognitive therapy.

Windy Dryden: What occasioned that interest?

John Marzillier: Well, I came to Oxford in 1982. Having gone from the Maudsley, I went to Birmingham and was working as a behaviour therapist in an academic psychology department. But then I moved to a job in the health service at Oxford, which is one of the places, as you know, where Beck's cognitive therapy has flourished in terms of research and training. So I took advantage of the presence of people like John Teasdale and Melanie Fennell, people I admired and respected and who were interested in cognitive therapy. I too became very interested in this approach. Beck (1970) had compared it with behaviour therapy, and I saw a lot of similarities between them.

Windy Dryden: Was that a natural shift?

John Marzillier: It fitted in with the academic study that I had done up to that date, which was in cognitive–behaviour therapy, so here was an approach which was quite explicitly 'cognitive'.

Windy Dryden: It was also seeming to parallel the developments in the field generally. So up to now your professional self-view, if you like, had really run alongside the development in the field as a whole.

John Marzillier: Yes.

Windy Dryden: From behaviour therapy, to cognitive–behaviour therapy, and thence to cognitive therapy.

John Marzillier: But another important input that influenced my views was my experience with clients. If you are at all open-minded, then any closed system of therapy becomes difficult to practise. For example, I saw many people who did not respond well to behavioural methods and these people taught me many things about the therapeutic process. In this context, I keep coming back to one particular case, actually the first patient I ever saw as a trainee therapist at the Maudsley. He was a young medical student who had a difficulty urinating in public. He was already in treatment with another trainee, carrying out systematic desensitisation, and I took over – it was as though you could exchange therapists, it didn't matter, you see.

Windy Dryden: One white coat was the same as another.

John Marzillier: Exactly. I was supervised by Jack Rachman and I followed Wolpe's technique very carefully, as one does with one's first case. And Jack was a very good supervisor, yet we didn't seem to get very far in terms of client improvement. The therapy was carried out initially in imagination, using relaxation and the usual procedures, and then I sought to transfer it to real life by setting up little situations in the Institute of Psychiatry. The client would use the toilet and someone would deliberately come in. But still there was very little progress. So we decided to meet nearer to his place of work, in a pub. I didn't think anything odd in this. I really wasn't aware that for some therapists this would be regarded as rather unusual behaviour; it seemed to me to be perfectly natural. The client, who was almost exactly my age, and I would meet in the pub and have a pint of beer, which would help him to use the toilet effectively. But you need time for that to take effect. So we had to spend about 40 minutes in the pub, drinking a pint of beer and chatting, and during that time he began to open up to me more about his own uncertainties about medicine as a career. He emerged as a rather lonely individual, someone who was quite ambitious for himself, and from a family that hadn't been very warm. This just came out in conversation. I didn't use it at all therapeutically at the time. I didn't even think of it in therapeutic terms.

Windy Dryden: It was just preparing him to go into the loo and to urinate.

John Marzillier: Absolutely. Eventually he made a little bit more progress, but not very much. The crunch came because he decided to leave his medical studies and go to India. This was not discussed in therapy at all, he just said one day that he was going to do this. I asked him what he felt about his problem, because it seemed to be rather a restriction to go to India when you have difficulty in urinating in public! Obviously it had gone completely from the top of his mental agenda right down to the bottom. He was so determined to go to India that it ceased to be a problem, which was interesting. And so he went to India, and I didn't see him again for something like two years. I met him by accident in the street in Camden Town, where I was living at the time. A car stopped and out got a self-confident young man, very different from the man I had seen before. He came up to me and asked me how I was, and said that he had been to India and had come back. So I asked him what he was doing now, thinking he had embarked on some esoteric career. 'Oh, I'm back on my medical studies, and I'm really enjoying it.' He was about to get into the car and I said, 'What about the problem?'. And I promise you, he said, 'What problem?'. He had totally forgotten! And I said, 'The problem of urinating in public'. 'Oh, that? Well, I still have that, but it doesn't bother me very much at all.' And that case has stuck with me, and I have come back to it because it has taught me a lot about what is important in therapy: the importance of the therapeutic relationship, of looking at the person as a whole and in the context of his or her life.

Windy Dryden: But did it teach you that at that time?

John Marzillier: No, not at that time, not consciously, anyway. It was only by thinking back over it. I suppose it made me think that doing behaviour therapy wasn't as simple as the textbooks might indicate. I was aware of that, but what the processes were, I could only come to later on as I began to study them more and became more aware of them from other patients and from other people I talked to.

Windy Dryden: So this was your first case, but one that you have come back to in your thinking several times.

John Marzillier: Yes. It makes me aware of issues like 'What is the problem?', 'How do you define it?', 'The importance of the therapeutic relationship' and 'The role of the age and gender of the therapist'. There's also the question of the choice of one's career and the impact that can have on the rest of one's life and the question of what people seek from therapy, what it is they want and what it is they gain. Perhaps that client gained quite a lot from the process of therapy, but perhaps not specifically from what we were doing.

Windy Dryden: Let's come back to your own development. So far we have reached the point where you are in Oxford, it's 1982 and you're doing cognitive therapy.

John Marzillier: I should also say that I began to be interested again in the dynamic approaches at the same time, but cognitive therapy struck me as being of particular interest because I thought it might marry some of the strengths of the more enlightened behavioural approaches with an explicit emphasis on cognitions. So I became very interested in cognitive therapy and felt that this was the therapy that I wanted to pursue. But my experience was very different. During my supervision and training, I became increasingly aware that this approach wasn't right; there was something missing. In the end I identified it as the fact that cognitive therapy adopted an excessively rationalistic approach. When I talked and wrote to Beck about this, he quickly dropped the term 'rational' and in fact at one stage claimed that the term 'rational' wasn't really his term. In fact I think it was, it was part of the American tradition which stressed a rational, scientific approach, but with the focus on cognition rather than on behaviour. But there seemed to be something missing. The essence of cognitive therapy according to Beck, and in this I felt he was right, was changing beliefs or assumptions. But it seemed to me that beliefs or assumptions were precisely the things that *didn't* change by the application of a Socratic method or by rational argument.

A case I had under supervision at the time epitomises this. I was seeing a man, who was mildly depressed when I saw him, who had been severely depressed several times and was very much a loner. Using cognitive therapy, I worked on his depression, identifying and challenging negative thoughts and trying to get to his underlying assumptions. We identified an assumption he held about himself: that he was inferior to other people, that people didn't consider him as important as them. He believed that this was epitomised by the fact that he hadn't received a renewal of his membership of the tennis club that he played at. He believed the club did not want him. So I thought I would tackle this in a cognitive way. I asked him to generate other explanations about why he had not received the renewal. He had great difficulty doing this but eventually we looked at a number of possibilities. It might have been held up in the post, or it might have got lost. I got him to test these out empirically by ringing up the membership secretary of the club. He discovered that there had been a mix-up at the printers and the renewal forms hadn't yet been printed. He received a form about a week later and this disconfirmed his hypothesis. He had received actual concrete disconfirmation. Now, did this change his belief about himself? Well, no, it didn't. Even though he acknowledged that he had not been rejected by the club, he *still* thought the people at this tennis club didn't really consider him the right sort of person to join. So the rational/empirical approach hadn't disconfirmed his fundamental belief in his inferiority to others. And this convinced me that an approach which stayed at this rather rational–empirical–scientific level wasn't the right way for changing such beliefs.

I had begun to read more widely, and people like Mike Mahoney and others brought to my attention the importance of tacit knowledge, tacit change – emotional factors which had been secondary, I felt, in the cognitive therapy approach. (At that stage, anyway; maybe it has changed now.) So that was my experience. I had entered into this therapy thinking, this is it, this seems very exciting. And yet I came away almost immediately from my experience with patients (and it wasn't just him but other patients too) with severe doubts. I asked my supervisors whether they had had any really positive experiences of changing dysfunctional beliefs, and in all honesty at that point they said they too had had great difficulty in changing dysfunctional beliefs by cognitive therapy methods. That was the most difficult area in which to effect change, and it appeared that cognitive therapy did not deliver the goods.

Windy Dryden: So then that prompted you to go back to your original interest, which was in the dynamic therapies.

John Marzillier: I was very fortunate because Anthony Storr (Consultant Psychotherapist at that time at the Warneford Hospital, where I worked) is a very approachable man, and he always liked people from different backgrounds to come along. I told him I was interested in dynamic psychotherapy and discussed it with him. He recommended a psychotherapist who I could see for personal therapy and also I took a case on, under his supervision, for dynamic psychotherapy. I began to read around the subject and began exploring this seemingly different approach, and that's how it started. Then eventually a course was put on at the Warneford, a general psychotherapy course, part-time for two years, which had as its major starting point, the analytic tradition and dynamic psychotherapy. It was a course for experienced therapists from different professional backgrounds, and I joined that course.

Windy Dryden: It sounds like what you were looking for at that point was the answer to the question of 'How can you help people to make more fundamental changes in themselves?'.

John Marzillier: Yes, that's what always interested me, both about myself and also about the people I worked with. That's one thing about staying in the same place for a long time. Your patients come back to you. There were a number of people I had seen in Oxford and in Birmingham too, for behavioural approaches, who did very well initially but 'relapsed', and so came back. I asked myself why and I always came back to the need for a more fundamental way of looking at their problems. Agoraphobics are a good case in point because the behavioural approach is very straightforward and apparently very successful. You can get agoraphobics to go out reasonably successfully by straightforward behavioural programmes. But that does not address some of the more fundamental things like difficulties of self-esteem, dependence, independence and marital relationships. These were the issues that Goldstein and Chambless (1978) wrote about in their very interesting paper. This would explain why you could make some improvement with behavioural methods, but relapses occurred. I became interested in finding something that was a bit more substantial, but that nevertheless was built upon the strengths of the pragmatic behavioural approach, because these are valuable and I don't want to lose them. Having done dynamic therapy, having read widely in psychoanalysis, I have also seen some of the worst sides of that, too, which is the excessive interest in and dependence on speculation, inference and subjectivity.

Windy Dryden: That kind of faith that you were asked to have at the Tavistock.

John Marzillier: Everybody knows the worst sort of the dynamic therapists – where everything is subject to an interpretation. That is not the way
to do analytic therapy appropriately. The best analysts like Patrick Case-
ment, Peter Lomas and others clearly don't do that, but that side of it does
exist. So that's why I'm interested in integration, in a way, because I have
experienced some of the benefits of pragmatic behavioural therapy, yet I am
very interested in the uncovering and explanation that goes on in dynamic
therapy. The question I have come to is whether one can marry those
approaches successfully or not.

Windy Dryden: Before we answer that question, let's go back to your
experience of being trained in analytic therapy and some of your experiences of practising that approach. Did it really give you the answer to your
question in terms of bringing about more fundamental attitude change?

John Marzillier: No, I don't think it has given me the answer, but I feel a
bit more comfortable with the approach to the answer. I think that in a way
the questions are very difficult, complicated questions. They are really the
questions that all of us address, whatever our experience and background,
and wherever we come from. So I don't expect the answers as I perhaps
expected them when I was younger. I have learnt that you often don't get
the answers, but the method, the approach, is important in itself. I think I
am also marrying things which suit my style and personality as a therapist.
For example, I think I am more comfortable with an intuitive approach and
a more verbal approach as well. Now, there are limitations to that, but it
suits me and I work better in that way.

Windy Dryden: One of the debates in the field of integration and eclecti-
cism at the moment is: At what level does one integrate? Now, clearly we
have been talking about the level of practice. How about the level of theory?
Are you also trying to integrate the theoretical underpinnings of behavioural, cognitive and dynamic therapies?

John Marzillier: Well, it sounds a very ambitious thing to do, doesn't it? I
am aware of areas where there is a theoretical convergence, particularly in
cognitive psychology. When I studied academic psychology, there wasn't
such a thing as cognitive psychology; there were different topics like
perception, memory etc. Now there is a huge area of cognitive psychology
and, although I can't profess to be an expert in it, some of it is about
dynamic processes such as repression and defence mechanisms. One of the
Portuguese Psychologists, Bara (1984) wrote that psychological processes
are predominantly unconscious. The conscious part of these processes is
only a small part, the tip of the iceberg, as it were. So you could say that
both cognitive and dynamic psychotherapy made me realise that a lot of
the processes that go on in any interchange, and in therapy in particular,
are unconscious processes. And what we do, through our expression, in

our language and in our contact with other people, is make them conscious. But the process of change is unconscious. Now that is a very exciting, very interesting and difficult area. If you read the history of the analytic approach (for example in Ellenberger's (1970) monumental tome, *The Discovery of the Unconscious*), you realise that there was a tremendous leap in the nineteenth century away from the old enlightenment ideas (where humans are presented as rational beings). What Freud did was to reverse that trend and point out how much of human behaviour is irrational and unconscious. This seems to be recognised now in cognitive psychology too.

Windy Dryden: One of the personal elements of this interview for me is, and I think you remember this quite well, that you have actually taught me behaviour therapy when I was a trainee counsellor at Aston University in the mid-1970s. Just listening to you at the moment and thinking about the John Marzillier I knew then, I was thinking, if John Marzillier then could hear John Marzillier speak in the vein you are talking now, would he have believed it possible?

John Marzillier: Well, I don't know the answer to that one, it's an impossible question to answer. And I think the answer is probably yes and no! The persona that I had at that time would say 'no', and put forward arguments against it. Certainly I was very strongly committed to a behavioural approach and saw it in contradistinction to the dynamic approach. But I think another part of me, perhaps represented in terms of unconscious processes, would have stated, 'Yes, I really am interested'.

Windy Dryden: Because at that time you came over in terms of your persona as a very committed behaviour therapist.

John Marzillier: Absolutely. I was, and I very much valued, and to a certain extent value now, the practical therapeutic approaches that went under that heading.

Windy Dryden: But it sounds as if your integration is still developing and you're still in a sense exploring that, at both a practical and a theoretical level.

John Marzillier: Yes, I think that the theoretical level is very difficult. I gave a talk in Dumfries on the relationship between cognitive and dynamic therapies, and I chose to do that predominantly at a theoretical level. It proved to be a very difficult talk. Someone in the audience said to me, 'Why are you interested in integration?', and I couldn't answer that question. It just seemed to me important and I am still not sure why I am interested in integration. I know that I am, and I suppose it might reflect something about my personality. One of the consequences of having dipped one's toe in the analytic water is that you become aware of the possible motivations for your interest in all sorts of areas. So it may be something to do with me and my background.

Windy Dryden: It sounds like you haven't yet discovered the reasons why you are interested in integration. You realise that you are, but you can't articulate those reasons at the moment.

John Marzillier: Not in any sensible way.

Windy Dryden: Just changing track – in terms of this professional journey – first of all, did it have any personal and professional costs for you, moving from a fairly traditional behavioural approach to a more dynamic, and now we discover a more integrative, approach? Did it lose you any professional or even personal friends along the way?

John Marzillier: It didn't lose me any friends. I have lost some contacts. I know that if I'd stayed within behaviour therapy I might have gone on perhaps to greater eminence within that approach. Some of my former colleagues may think that I have reneged on the applied scientist model, on the principles that led to the development of the behavioural approach, although I don't think I have. I prefer to see myself as having found other, equally important principles to complement the scientific ones. But I certainly have not experienced any hostility or rejection. Quite the contrary. I still maintain close ties with friends within the behavioural therapy movement. If you talk to most behaviour therapists, you will find that they are nowhere near as narrow-minded as people believe. The development of cognitive therapy, for example, has opened up the whole field, and, as I said earlier, anyone who is truly open-minded and has practised therapy for several years must realise that no one school of therapy has all the answers.

Windy Dryden: Where do you go from here? Where will your interest in the integrative approach take you?

John Marzillier: That's hard to say. From a personal point of view I would like to develop the creative side of my work. George Kelly wrote of the person as a scientist and, as you know, applied it to everyone, clients and therapists alike. You might invert this maxim and think of the scientist as a person, applying this idea to those of us who, under the banner of science, seek greater knowledge of the world and of people. We should not lose touch with the personal, subjective, human side of ourselves. This can be a source of creativity and ultimately, I believe, wisdom. It can also help us to become better therapists. Miller Mair (1989) has expounded these ideas very persuasively in his latest book. I would like to spend more time on understanding the *processes* of change and I hope that in doing so I can both learn more about myself as well as become a more helpful therapist.

Windy Dryden: Thank you very much, John.

References

BARA, B.G. (1984). Modifications of knowledge by memory processes. In M. A. Reda and M. J. Mahoney (eds), *Cognitive Psychotherapies*. Cambridge, MA: Ballinger.

BECK, A.T. (1970). Cognitive therapy: Nature and relation to behavior therapy. *Behavior Therapy* 1, 184–200.

ELLENBERGER, H. (1970). *The Discovery of the Unconscious*. London: Allen & Unwin.

GOLDSTEIN, A.J. and CHAMBLESS, D. (1978). A reanalysis of agoraphobia. *Behavior Therapy* 9, 47–59.

MAIR, M. (1989). *Between Psychology and Psychotherapy. A Poetics of Experience*. London: Routledge.

Chapter 9
The Counsellor and ME
An Interview with Pat Milner

Pat Milner was born in Lancashire, attended Bolton School and was trained first as a teacher in Liverpool and then as a school counsellor. After working as a school counsellor in a Hampshire comprehensive school, and feeling in need of further learning in this new, pioneering area, she became a Fulbright Scholar at the State University of New York at Buffalo, where she worked with students, and studied for a Master's degree. On her return, University College London advertised for its first student counsellor and because she had enjoyed working with students and had just learned about the College through hearing its Provost speaking in America, she applied for the post, got the job and started work in London in 1969.

The next 6 years were an almost non-stop kaleidoscope of demands, challenges and mind-expanding experiences, including starting a new service in a defensive centre of excellence; working with some outstanding colleagues to create the Association for Student Counselling; and being invited to write a book to share knowledge and experience. For Pat, this was a rich time of alarms and excursions, of naïve choices and actions, of meetings of minds from all over the world, and incredible learning. The security of her cottage in Hampshire and the family it housed were painfully sacrificed. Living in London was part of that 6-year experience, and then a move out to Petersfield and daily commuting once more.

The link between UCL and the South West London College Counselling Course, which was the focus of the next 6 years of Pat's career, was, in Pat's words, 'provided by a young man who applied for a placement in the Counselling Service at UCL whilst doing his PhD in Psychology and training at South West London College. Dr Windy Dryden is once again the link man in that he conducted the following interview', . . . an interview which starts at this point in Pat's biographical history. Here the years from the mid-1970s to the present are explored with the focus being on Pat's experience of ME (myalgic encephalomyelitis) and its impact on her personal and professional life.

Windy Dryden: In this interview, Pat, I would like to explore with you your experience of suffering from myalgic encephalomyelitis, or what is more commonly known as ME. I believe that you first discovered you were suffering from ME in 1976. How did you find that out?

Pat Milner: When I look back to that time, just looking at my life in general, from about 1965 I had been one of a small group of people who had been sort of driving a pioneering track through what now looks like an educational jungle. We were working to introduce the concept and the practice of counselling into comprehensive schools, and then at college and university level. I had done a lot of work, being founder Chair of the Association for Student Counselling, trying with others to create a supporting group for counsellors and an organisation that would help to promote counselling, which was really a very new American, and therefore not very English, way of helping people to help themselves. I had written one of the first English books on the subject of counselling in education. And almost as an afterthought I had two major operations. So looking back to that time of 1976 and the years that preceded it, they really had been quite hectic.

After leaving UCL in 1975 I took a temporary post for a year, lecturing in education at Goldsmiths' College. I was living in Petersfield and commuting daily to south-east London. The spring term was a teaching practice term, which meant visiting students in London schools. Towards the end of February I was completely laid low with a bad attack of 'flu which so completely took the legs from under me, that it was difficult even to get out of bed to go to the bathroom and I didn't go out of my flat for three weeks. That left me feeling quite fragile. But I was gradually able to get out and about, and was left with what seemed to be a very intractable stiff neck. It didn't respond to physiotherapy at the hospital. It got worse and worse and gradually the pain seemed to spread from my neck into my shoulders, into my arms, into my back and legs, until my whole body was in pain. A local consultant diagnosed this as post-viral rheumatism, and that was my first diagnosis. The first diagnosis wasn't actually ME, but it was a post-viral illness and the prognosis was that it would burn itself out in 2 years.

But in addition to seeing that consultant, I saw privately, through a good friend, quite a wise osteopath and doctor, to try and get some help with the pain. And he advised me to give up work completely, to rest, even if that meant going back to living in a bedsit. He said what I needed was complete rest, but really the price felt too high to me. After all the years that had gone into getting my nice flat, I just couldn't cope with the idea of giving it all up, so I compromised by taking a year off full-time work, during which I did a short lecture tour of South African universities, against medical advice, some part-time training work at South West London College and had six months just pottering.

Windy Dryden: So you knew that something had to change radically, but you didn't want to go the drastic route that that wise doctor suggested to you.

Pat Milner: I couldn't face that, although in retrospect it would probably have been a good idea. I did what I could face, which was to compromise, take some time off, and get very much better. I had a lovely summer of playing in the country, going down to the sea and doing bits of work, and generally relaxing, and that had a good effect. So by September 1977 I went back to full-time work. This time it was at South West London College, working with the counselling course team.

Windy Dryden: So you had a year where you were working under half or quarter steam.

Pat Milner: Yes, very much so. Or even no steam at all.

Windy Dryden: But in 1977 you felt ready enough to go back into full time work.

Pat Milner: Yes, I did. It was a new job. It was training on a particularly attractive kind of course, a self-directed learning community with a very supportive group of people. And that seemed a good direction to move in. Still in counselling, although not in actual counselling work, but training other pepole.

Windy Dryden: And then what happened?

Pat Milner: I went back to full-time work and it actually worked quite well for a time. But then, because I am a workaholic, the old demon took over and I found that I was doing more or less what I had done before, putting all my energy and efforts into work. It was very rewarding work, very enjoyable, but on a very creative course which had the stresses and tension of being run in a fairly typical educational institution and the structure that goes with that. It was also a very itinerant course which moved home regularly every year or two years to whatever premises in central London we could find.

Windy Dryden: Which must have added to the stress.

Pat Milner: Yes. So there was excitement, there was support, there was a lot of good learning. But there was also stress and hard work, both there and in my home life. What gradually happened to me over that period until about 1983 was that the symptoms came back and I slowly got less and less able to manage physically, and became quite shut-down emotionally.

Windy Dryden: So the job sounds as if it demanded a high level of energy, and you were gradually realising that your energy was becoming more and more drained again.

Pat Milner: Yes, that's right. And it was hard for me to accept that I could no longer be the sort of busy, hardworking person that I always had been. But in a way my body would no longer do what I wanted it to do. Having served me magnificently practically all my life, and done everything that I asked of it, playing sport, walking in the Lake District, decorating my home, dashing around here and there, it would no longer do it. It was as if my body said to me: 'Stop it. I can't go on carrying you around, living the life that you are living.'

Windy Dryden: So having had to accept reluctantly the grim reality that your body wouldn't serve you in the way your mind wanted it to, what happened then?

Pat Milner: Then I retired on grounds of ill health from South West London College. That was in 1983, and for three years I didn't work at all. So from 1977, where I had got better in a year, this time it was three years of pottering about, before I felt well enough and pain-free enough to think about working again.

Windy Dryden: At what point did you receive the diagnosis of ME?

Pat Milner: Well, that diagnosis came about 1987.

Windy Dryden: So it was after you retired.

Pat Milner: Yes, the grounds on which I retired were post-viral rheumatism.

Windy Dryden: You still had the same, original diagnosis.

Pat Milner: Yes, that's right.

Windy Dryden: Was it a relief for you to discover that you were suffering from ME?

Pat Milner: It was a mixture of things, really. I mean, everybody knows about rheumatism, it's been around for a long time, it's a word that people know, it's an illness that people know. ME is something that people don't know. What is this peculiar illness, with this funny name that is so difficult that you have to spell it out? So in some senses it was more difficult to have that diagnosis than the other one. But in other ways it made more sense of what was happening to me, because there was nothing in what I knew about post-viral rheumatism that accounted for not only what had happened to my body but what had happened to me as a person, as a result of this illness. When my body revolted, as it were, my mind and my personality were really quite gob-smacked. My mind couldn't make decisions, my body had gone on strike, and my personality and my emotions wandered about like a lost child, between a body that wouldn't work and a mind that wouldn't work either, and couldn't think. And that made me feel totally different.

Windy Dryden: So you must have wondered where this energetic, work-aholic Pat Milner had gone to?

Pat Milner: Exactly. Where had she gone? She wasn't here any more, so in a way it was a change of personality. And I think that is one of the most difficult things for people to understand. I think people don't understand the illness. They don't understand the extreme fatigue that the illness brings. They're inclined to be sceptical and say either that it doesn't exist at all as an illness – that people are perhaps malingering – or that they are hysterical.

Windy Dryden: Did you experience that personally?

Pat Milner: Yes, and no. My wise doctor in 1977 and my own GP have been very faithful in their support, but I was on invalidity and sickness benefit for a while, and the people who were most sceptical were of course the DSS, particularly the medical people. They found it very difficult to understand that you could actually do all their little tests with your muscles, because you can work for a short time; it's prolonged activity that causes you to relapse, as it were. So the most scepticism came from them. So that's part of the medical profession. Also from people like a rheumatologist at Guy's, who said, 'No, this illness doesn't exist, what you've got is not organic'.

Windy Dryden: It's in the mind.

Pat Milner: That's it. It's depression, for example.

Windy Dryden: How did you react to this form of scepticism?

Pat Milner: It's confusing, because you can't help thinking that if some-body like a doctor says, 'No, it's not that, it's this', then they should know, really, because they're the doctors, the medical people. They are trained in this, they should know about it; that's my strong childhood indoctrination. So you feel quite confused and really disbelieve the evidence of your own body, mind and spirit. From feeling quite negated and therefore losing a lot of confidence in myself, I swung to the other extreme, which was to feel quite hostile and sceptical sometimes towards the medical profession. You know, unless you have got a boil on the end of your nose, they're not going to know what's wrong with you. I would swing from one extreme to the other. Either they were totally right and I was a complete mess, or they couldn't see what was wrong with you unless it was painfully obvious.

Windy Dryden: So it was a black and white thing for you either way. Now, I understand that you came out of retirement in 1986, but that you didn't go straight back into counselling as a career.

Pat Milner: That's right.

Windy Dryden: Why not?

Pat Milner: I didn't think I could do it.

Windy Dryden: The old Pat Milner really had gone.

Pat Milner: Yes, she had. All that pioneering spirit had gone. I just didn't feel confident, I didn't feel capable of working with other people in this very personal and quite close way, which is reliant upon concentration and memory, neither of which can be relied on by those with ME.

Windy Dryden: Did you feel it might be too draining for you?

Pat Milner: Yes, it might be too draining. I thought I wouldn't be effective. I felt I couldn't possibly be effective, given the *me* that was available. So what I did was to go back to a type of work that was near to things I had done before, by becoming a training officer on the Isle of Dogs. I wanted to work locally to Greenwich, because travelling is not easy – it's still not easy for me – and went to work with a community programme, doing training which I knew a bit about. Training doesn't involve you in close one-to-one personal contact with people. It does sometimes, but generally speaking it's not as close in the work you do as counselling is.

Windy Dryden: And therefore not as draining?

Pat Milner: That's right. Then I became the manager of that community programme after a couple of months. I enjoyed that and I did regain a lot of confidence, but found that the full-time work was too much for me, so after a year I went to work, part-time this time, again fairly locally in Forest Hill, working in a voluntary care centre. So again, it was not counselling, but work that was helping people, working with volunteers, working in the community, which I always think is important. So it was a job that fulfilled some of the things that I think are important, and some of the things I felt capable of doing. But it really was there that I became more and more inclined to want to help people in a counselling way again. So after two years, that's what I decided to do – to go freelance and to see what I could do in terms of counselling, supervising counsellors and training counsellors.

Windy Dryden: And that's what you are doing now.

Pat Milner: That's what I am doing now, on a part-time basis.

Windy Dryden: So that brings us up to date. Looking back on your experience with ME, what would you say you have learned from it as a person?

Pat Milner: I have learned not to take my body for granted, and to take better care of it than I used to. It is human and fallible, it's not a machine, but it is a good barometer. That's been very important. I have learned to work with people in a way that is more economical of my resources. I have always counselled in quite an intuitive way, and have used that intuition to get in touch with people at quite a deep level – a level that went far beyond words. It's a very vital way of working but one which is also over a long period a very draining way of working, too. And almost without realising it, working in that way would drain my energies and resources, so my work now is less intuitive and in a way slightly more cognitive. I use my mind more.

Windy Dryden: We've discussed your experience of ME and the history of it, in terms of the effect it has had on you as a person. Now let's move on to look at the relationship between having ME and doing counselling. You are saying that you have to keep your intuition under some kind of check.

Pat Milner: Yes, that is what I feel.

Windy Dryden: The fear is that if you really gave full rein to it, you would overly stretch yourself again.

Pat Milner: Intuition is a very powerful gift; it can, if you like, burn you out and I think that is part of what happened to me. By using it alongside other skills, talents, in a more equal way, then I can survive so much better.

Windy Dryden: So in a sense, it is putting the intuition in its place with a range of other skills and talents. Perhaps in the past you really gave *full* rein to your intuition.

Pat Milner: Yes, I think I over-developed that sensitivity.

Windy Dryden: Although that enabled you to work at a deep level, and was presumably helpful for your clients, it had its long-term toll on you.

Pat Milner: Yes, the cost was very high.

Windy Dryden: So you have learned to pace yourself more, I guess.

Pat Milner: Yes, which is what is happening now in this interview. I am slowing down, making shorter responses and recouping some energy.

Windy Dryden: What else have you learned from ME in terms of your counselling work?

Pat Milner: I have learned yet again that my counselling work needs to be fed by other things. For example, one of the things that I did when I retired was to join a choir. I started to sing, which was something I had enjoyed in the past and although, or perhaps because, I sing with more enthusiasm than talent it is very therapeutic. The choir is a major point in my week; in some ways it comes first. And this is something I have internalised, at least – not always to put the work first, but to put the things that help me and therefore the work first. Like looking after me. I still slip very badly and get the old workaholic demon back again, but the work ethic is much less powerful, thankfully.

Windy Dryden: Would you say that the experience of having ME has enriched your counselling work in any way?

Pat Milner: It has brought more of a tolerance for, if you like, the more ordinary and everyday difficulties that people encounter, which I was not exactly intolerant of, but which didn't always seem as important as some of the deeper things that people struggled with. And I think now that they are, because they affect more people and they are difficulties for me now. People who struggle deeply with their lives are fewer in number, and my own struggles are more practical and physical, and thus more in balance with emotional and philosophical issues.

Windy Dryden: I guess that is what is called 'hassles' in the psychological literature.

Pat Milner: Yes, that's right. Yes.

Windy Dryden: You have realised that that is an important level to work at with people.

Pat Milner: Because I had ignored the cost of the hassles of my own life. I had over-ridden them. And because I can't do that now, I have become much more aware of the difficulties that other people have in doing that. I don't know whether that makes any sense.

Windy Dryden: Let's see if I can express that in the way it is coming over to me. Prior to having ME, when you were fully functioning at quite a deep level yourself, your intuition led you to be in touch with the deeper issues of people's lives. Perhaps in doing that you didn't pay as much attention as you do now to the hassles of people's lives. Now having had the personal experience of those hassles yourself, it has in a sense made you appreciate more the effect of those hassles on your clients' lives.

Pat Milner: Yes, that's it.

Windy Dryden: Let's move on to what we can learn from your experience which might help counsellors working with clients with ME in their practice.

Pat Milner: I think it is important to take ME seriously. In fact the ME Action Campaign has a little car sticker which I have on the back of my car, and it says 'Take ME seriously'. It is not a fatal illness, but it is an illness that changes your life so totally that it's crucial to recognise that this is what happens to people. It is also helpful not to take it so seriously that you become its helpless victim. It is an illness that makes you feel a victim, and you are indeed a victim in lots of ways. But it's important to realise that it is an illness that you learn to *manage* as best you can, rather than let it manage you. Because if you let it manage you, you can become really quite disabled, and you can't overcome that disability just by an act of willpower – you do need quite a lot of support.

Windy Dryden: In fact the act of willpower can be draining in itself.

Pat Milner: Yes. You can benefit from the support of somebody who does understand that although this illness debilitates you, at the same time there is still some of you there that wants to get back into the mainstream of everyday life in whatever ways you can. You still want to have some achievements that you can manage. They won't be the same as the ones you could manage before, but there are still things you can do and enjoy, and feel satisfaction in. You are not a mindless cabbage, which is what you feel sometimes. And it is something about hope and travelling hopefully in what feels an essentially hopeless life. Counsellors need to support people to find out what they can do and who they are now. People know what they can't do when they have got ME. It's finding out what you can do and who you can be that seems so important, and this is best done by trying things gently.

Windy Dryden: So first of all, take ME seriously and learn about the effects it can have on people. Gently counter the hopelessness that can easily be engendered, and encourage people to focus on what they can do instead of dwelling on what they can't do; but in a way that doesn't shift the person into willpower mode.

Pat Milner: Yes.

Windy Dryden: Is there also something about pacing the work with clients with ME in the sense of realising perhaps that, because of the debilitating nature of the illness, work at a deep level might be draining for them, and perhaps therefore contraindicated?

Pat Milner: Yes. It's always important to follow the client in counselling, but with a client with ME you have got to follow in a slightly different way. They may, for example, not be able to have an hour's counselling session because an hour can be too long for them. So what about half an hour? Whatever works and is helpful in that sense. ME forces people to change life patterns and provides an opportunity to review things, but their energy reserves are so low that the intellectual and emotional stamina needed are only available for short and unpredictable periods, and it may be that there is a case for considering visiting ME clients in their homes. Travel, and getting about can be extremely difficult for them. Some counsellors would find that this was something they wouldn't want to do. They would rather have clients either on their own territory or on neutral ground. But I wonder if having visiting counsellors would help. Not just for people with ME either, but for people with any kind of debilitating illness or condition. There are more serious disabilities than ME that we can learn from. The Macmillan nurses who visit those with cancer are an example. Each person's experience of ME is individual and needs to be approached in that way – we are looking now at the general patterns.

Windy Dryden: So you are advocating the importance of flexibility.

Pat Milner: Yes, a re-think. Yes, flexibility. Not compromising your own principles as a counsellor, but bending them perhaps a little bit in a way that doesn't do violence to your own beliefs but which enables you to work flexibly with your client.

Windy Dryden: We spoke earlier of the scepticism that you encountered mainly from the medical profession. My knowledge of people with ME is that they do find quite wide scepticism among friends, family and business associates, as well as the medical profession. From your experience, how might counsellors help their ME clients deal with this?

Pat Milner: I think it is very difficult because what the scepticism does is negate anything that you might use to deal with it. It makes you feel quite confused, quite despairing and angry. I suppose, really, some of the assertion skills could be helpful in that they enable you to say what's going on for you and to be able to stay with that. And not to get pushed away from it by other people's disbelief or scepticism. Group support can be crucially strengthening, and perhaps to practise with clients in the counselling sessions ways in which they might deal with people they encounter at work and in their families. Things like that which can bring some confirmation of worth and some support because it is an illness that makes you feel devastatingly alone sometimes. The ME experience can be so impossible to grasp and convey that you feel that nobody could possibly understand, particularly if your family or close friends don't understand; people who – say, if you had a broken leg – bring round a bunch of flowers, and sign your plaster cast, and be generally accepting of it.

Windy Dryden: There is nothing to sign when you have ME, is there?

Pat Milner: No, there isn't. In that sense I suppose it is a bit like other invisible illnesses that are more in the mental health area, which you can't see or sign. People with ME do get very depressed. I don't think the depression causes the ME. I do think it's the other way round. But the person with ME who is depressed needs the same help as any other person with depression might need, both physically and psychologically, within his or her individual experience.

Windy Dryden: So in a sense the assertion skills would enable the person to develop that car sticker message – not only to take ME seriously, but to take *me* seriously.

Pat Milner: Yes, exactly.

Windy Dryden: Thank you very much.

Chapter 10
Therapists and the Whole Person

An Interview with John Rowan

John Rowan is the author of a number of books, including *The Reality Game: A Guide to Humanistic Counselling and Therapy* (Routledge, 1983), *The Horned God: Feminism and Men as Wounding and Healing* (Routledge, 1987), *Ordinary Ecstasy: Humanistic Psychology in Action* (2nd edition, Routledge, 1988) and *Subpersonalities* (Routledge, 1990). He has co-edited *Human Inquiry: A Sourcebook of New Paradigm Research* (Wiley, 1981) with Peter Reason, and *Innovative Therapy in Britain* (Open University Press, 1988) with Windy Dryden. He is at present writing a book on transpersonal psychotherapy for Routledge. He is on the Editorial Board of *Self and Society*, the *Journal of Humanistic Psychology* and the *Journal of Integrative and Eclectic Psychotherapy*. He is a founder member and current Chair of the Association of Humanistic Psychology Practitioners. He helps to produce the magazine *Achilles Heel*. He is a chartered psychologist (member of the Counselling Psychology Special Group and the Psychotherapy Section of the British Psychological Society), a qualified psychotherapist (AHPP) and an accredited counsellor (BAC). He practises primal integration, which is a holistic approach to therapy, and teaches at a number of different centres. His particular workshop interests are creativity, body languages (with Sue Mickleburgh), sexuality and sex roles (with Sue Mickleburgh), and subpersonalities. He lives with Sue Mickleburgh in Walthamstow, and has four children from a previous marriage.

His views on the completeness of the training needed for psychotherapy were largely formed within the training group led in the late 1970s by Bill Swartley, who laid stress on the four functions of Jung and regarded primal integration as an approach which could and did do justice to all of them. They were extended by his own spiritual development and his discovery of the work of Ken Wilber, which influenced him a great deal. He started putting forward the position in the early 1980s that psychotherapy was a natural bridge between psychology and spirituality, and an article of his saying as much was published in *New Forum* (the journal of the Psychology and Psychotherapy Association before it became the present *Changes*) in July 1982. This article finished with the words:

> Psychotherapy as Janus, then: one face pointing back to childhood and the repressions and hangups of the past; the other face pointing forward to spirituality and the divine. Something fundamentally ambiguous and hard to

contain. Something much more risky and dangerous than we had supposed. Something much more deep and wonderful than we had ever imagined.

It seems from this interview that he has not retracted these words or drawn back from this position.

Windy Dryden: In this interview, John, I want to explore with you your views on the contemporary scene in psychotherapy, to consider your view that we really do need to help the whole human being, and that most therapists fall short. So perhaps we can start with your view on the contemporary scene with respect to that point.

John Rowan: Well, the main point is the implicit promise of psychotherapy, which is that if you go into the process and follow it through, you will come out at the end a whole human being, like the human being that you were supposed to be in the first place and have somehow not been done justice to, for one reason or another, along the way. Most people get into therapy through some crisis or other that tells them that they are not getting it right, that they are somehow not the full person they hoped to be or thought they were, or whatever. They realise that some changes need to be made if they are going to get out of the current crisis and go on to a better place than they were in before. Because if they just get back to where they were before, then they are liable to fall into the same crisis again, or a similar crisis. So what has to happen is that they get *through* the crisis and into a process which will take them on to a level where they won't have that kind of crisis any more. And I think that the only way to do that ultimately is to do justice to that whole person, what Maslow calls self-actualisation, that is, being all that you have it in you to be, or being that self that you truly are. So it isn't a question of taking on things that you are lacking or adding or subtracting things or something like that. It's a question of a total transformation, a total change of personality or character. And it seems to me that the whole person must be involved in that. Now I think there are a lot of psychotherapies about which explicitly, consciously, deliberately ignore and do not do justice to large portions of the person. I mean portions of the person that are really important, and the most obvious of those and the most often ignored is the spiritual aspect of the person.

Windy Dryden: Now, by 'spiritual', you mean what?

John Rowan: Well, let me lead up to that by drawing attention to Jung's distinction between the four functions that everybody has: sensing, feeling, thinking and intuiting. This faculty of intuiting has a lot to do with a sense of the future, where you are going, and your direction, your purpose, and that sort of thing. If you do justice to it, it will take you into that spiritual area, and by 'spiritual' I mean that area which goes beyond the limitations of your ego *and* the limitations of your self (whatever conception of that self you might have). It goes beyond that. You are not going to be limited to that, there is more to a human being, as it were, than just being three-dimensional beings walking about on the face of the earth. There is something larger than that which we can do justice to.

Windy Dryden: Now, if we can talk quite specifically here for a moment, you are saying that quite a number of psychotherapies which are being practised today neglect the spiritual side of the person. Perhaps you can give a concrete example of work at a spiritual level that these contemporary psychotherapies wouldn't be able to address.

John Rowan: Well, for example, Dina Glouberman (1989) once mentioned a dream about getting lost on a train, which was perfectly dealable with in gestalt terms, and meant a lot to her personally and was a perfectly sound, sensible, existential message from her to herself. Then the next day she actually met a woman who had exactly the same problem that she had in the dream, and it was actually almost word-for-word the same as what had happened in the dream. Now, if she had told that to a therapist, a lot of therapists would say: 'Well, nothing much we can do with that, that's just a coincidence, let's go on to something more interesting.' But somebody who is tuned into the spiritual level would say: 'Well that's very interesting, it really means that your unconscious is actually reaching into the future, not just into the past and present, and if you cultivate that, and do justice to it, it could be of real use to you, it could be a talent, an ability you have which is natural to you, which some people haven't got, but which can be cultivated if we pay attention to it.' And I would say: 'Really take that seriously.'

Windy Dryden: Right. So you would say then that quite a number of contemporary approaches to psychotherapy wouldn't be working at that level. A therapist from those traditions just wouldn't know how to deal with it.

John Rowan: Yes, and this is not just in the spiritual area. I mentioned that because it's the most obvious one. The next most obvious one is work at the fetal level; work at what happened to us before we were born. And again, to give you a classic example, there is a book by David Malan (1979) called *Individual Psychotherapy and the Science of Psychodynamics.* He has a whole page there about a patient of his who had this dream which was full of umbilical imagery of tubes and liquids and exactly the kind of problems that I am very familiar with. Frank Lake wrote a lot about this under the heading of 'Umbilical affect' and he took it very seriously. Malan says, in effect: 'Well, of course you know there seems to be something about the womb, but we know that that can't possibly be so, so we'll interpret it as *oral* material.'

Windy Dryden: Right. So it was outside his range of convenience.

John Rowan: That's right. So he had to change it into something that was within his range of convenience. And this is what happens in therapy that doesn't do justice to certain areas of human experience. Because it doesn't come in their training or doesn't come in their frame of reference, they actually distort it, quite a lot of the time, into something they *can* understand, so that it *does* come within their frame of reference.

Windy Dryden: Right, so they are, in a sense, like Procrustes. They are distorting the experience so they can deal with it.

John Rowan: That's right. There is a beautiful book by Eileen Walkenstein (1975) called *Shrunk to Fit*, which is about Procrustes and about how a lot of psychiatrists and psychotherapists do exactly that. And she teaches you in the book how not to do it.

Windy Dryden: Now before we look at Rowan's Recipe for therapists who can work with people so that they can be whole human beings, why do you think the situation has come to pass that so many therapists, in your view, only deal with parts of a human being and not the full human being? How do you account for that?

John Rowan: Well, I think it's because it never came up in their training. Obviously you can push that back and back, but basically it wasn't in their training, and they are not acute enough or flexible enough to invent it. You see, Winnicott was an example of somebody who was sharp enough to invent things when necessary. Back in the 1940s he had a patient who wanted to crawl between his legs and be reborn, so he let him crawl between his legs and be reborn. He was flexible enough to do that.

Windy Dryden: He didn't interpret it as acting-out or whatever.

John Rowan: No. And it turned out to be extremely valuable for that person. But if you have to invent it every time, then it puts a lot of stress on you. Why shouldn't it be in the training in the first place?

Windy Dryden: OK. So what you seem to be saying is that apart from the few who are acute or sharp enough to invent things that are outside their range of convenience to help deal with material that the client needs to deal with, most therapists are like prisoners of their training. They have been trained presumably by trainers who are also limited, and therefore what you seem to be advocating is a sort of massive programme of training for elite therapists who can then work to help people to become whole human beings. Is that the Rowan image?

John Rowan: More than that. I think the suggestion is that trainers on training courses need to go in for a process of self-re-education, which they are always doing anyway. You see, people who are experienced and are training other people are always going to conferences, meetings and lectures, always reading books etc. So all it needs really is for them to take that a little more seriously and say: 'Here is an area where I am seriously lacking, I need to bone up on this.' And there needs to be short courses, or long courses, however long it needs to be, to enable people to do that re-training of themselves. Then they will be fit to teach.

Windy Dryden: OK. Let's have a look at Rowan's image of the Complete Therapist. What do you think therapists need in order to be able to work with the full range of human experience?

John Rowan: I think they need to be able to work with all nine of Ken Wilber's (1986) nine fulcrums that are laid out in his book *Transformations of Consciousness*.

Windy Dryden: OK. In general, what are these levels?

John Rowan: Well, Wilber says that a fulcrum, as he defines it, is a turning point in everybody's life, where they have to make a new differentiation, a new kind of self, a new kind of vision of the world. And he says there are two stages which everybody goes through at each fulcrum. One of the stages is starting on that path, and you can refuse to do that, dig in your heels and say, for whatever reason, 'I am not going to start on that next step'. Or you can go half way and then get scared, traumatised, upset or diverted, or whatever, and stop short at that point.

The first fulcrum is way back at the fetal level, the symbiotic level, where the differentiation you have to make is between your fantasy about yourself and your fantasies about the world. That's a very difficult dif-ferentiation to make when you haven't got language and you haven't got much to go on in the way of experience. So he says that if you go wrong on that one, what you get are autistic psychoses, the very hardest, deepest kind of psychoses, because they come from that very, very early differen-tiation that isn't happening. Then you go up to the next fulcrum and if that goes wrong you get schizophrenia, serious kinds of depressive psychosis and that sort of thing, which again are very hard to deal with because they go so far back. At the next fulcrum you get the narcissistic borderline disorders and so forth. At the next one you get the classic neuroses. With the next one you get what he calls 'script disorders', which TA [transactio-nal analysis] talks about. Then the next one he calls 'identity disorders', which have to be dealt with by a process of Socratic reasoning, not therapy as normally understood. Then the next one you get is the Centaur stage where you get specific neuroses to do with existential angst and stuff like that, which is very hard to handle. The next one you come to is the transpersonal, the subtle stage, and there you get specifically spiritual emergencies, invasions from outside, as it were, that are very hard to deal with. The next one you get on to is the causal stage, where you get what is called, I think, 'Arhat's disease'. So at every single fulcrum something can go wrong. Now you don't have to worry too much about the very highest levels. I wouldn't insist that every therapist was trained in how to deal with those kinds of disorders. Because you are not going to come across them that often.

The disorders you are going to have to deal with most of all are the classic neuroses and the script disorders, the sorts of things that are really very common, but you are going to have to be able to cope with the narcissistic and borderline stuff, and so on. You are going to have to be trained for that. But you are going to have to be able to cope with spiritual emergencies because they actually are happening more often now. That is occurring more often. So you are going to get that sort of problem.

Windy Dryden: It seems to me that there are two possibilities in approaching work across these levels. One would be – and I think this is the one you would advocate – that a given therapist should strive to work at each of these levels. The reason they can't at the moment is that they are a prisoner of their past training. They need to continue on a path of professional and self-development to enable them to do that. Now, another model seems to be that we say, 'OK, it's perhaps unrealistic to expect any given individual to do that. Maybe we need specialists'. That's the old idea that counsellors would work at one level, at the classic neurosis level, and if you find somebody who has a narcissistic or borderline personality disorder, refer them on to a psychotherapist, or refer them on to somebody who can actually work with them at that level. Now, what is your view of those two very different approaches to therapy provision and training of therapists?

John Rowan: I think they are both fine. What I object to is people who refuse to admit that there is anything other than what came up in their training. It's that kind of wilful neglect that I really hate.

Windy Dryden: Give me an example of that.

John Rowan: Well, there's a book by Albert Ellis and Ray Yeager (1989). What they do in that book is to say 'We don't have to bother about any of that spiritual stuff because it's all phoney stuff anyway, it's all ridiculous, and people who get into that area just talk nonsense'. And the way they do that is by misperceiving it, by putting together things that don't belong together. They lump together all kinds of phenomena and all kinds of people who hate each other's guts or have nothing much to do with each other. Or they don't make the necessary discriminations to sort out the field that they're talking about. So for them it becomes one vast mish-mash of codswallop, as it were, and so it is very easily dismissed. Whereas as soon as you start making those discriminations you find that there *are* charlatans at every level, there are phonies at every level. There are people who are kidding themselves and other people at every level.

Windy Dryden: But you would say that you don't have to dismiss the entire spectrum out of hand because of that.

John Rowan: No.

Windy Dryden: OK. So what you are saying is that you object to therapists who say, in effect, 'My training is sufficient, anything outside of that is really basically crap and bullshit, we don't have to worry about it; and if I had any clients coming up with that kind of stuff I would quickly try to disabuse them of it and work in my particular domain'. Have I understood you correctly?

John Rowan: Yes, that's exactly right. And I think that happens a lot.

Windy Dryden: Right. But we mentioned two routes, one route where as a single therapist you would embark upon quite a vast training enterprise, versus the idea where you train in a specific area and you know your strengths and limitations. What would your vision be about the development of psychotherapy in the future, if you had to choose between these two routes?

John Rowan: Well, ideally I would like everybody to do the whole job. I mean, that would be my ideal. I think realistically that would take too long and would be too demanding and too difficult. So I would say I have got perhaps my immediate demands, as it were, and my long-term strategy. I think the immediate demand would be for people to recognise their limitations, not to pooh-pooh things they haven't done themselves, and to know where to refer people who are dealing with stuff they can't cope with. That would be good enough for a sort of intermediate programme. But in the long run I would like to see far more dissatisfaction among psychotherapists about their own performance. I would like to see them really doubting whether their training has been good enough, and for a lot of re-training to be available. I would like, on every street corner, as it were, for there to be training courses for trainers.

Windy Dryden: Are you, then, picking up a kind of smugness about the field that says something like – 'Look, one version of the research literature says that we do a pretty good job. We help two out of three of the people who come to us, and there is not much difference between different approaches. We are actually doing quite a good job. We don't need to develop in this way'? Are you responding to that sort of smugness?

John Rowan: There is a smugness about that. I think there is a kind of digging in of your heels and saying: 'Look, I am not convinced that I need to change in any respect at all. I think I may not be able to do everything, but I do a pretty good job. My clients are satisfied, they don't want any more than that. If they could just get back to work or get back into their relationship or make a new relationship, then I am happy.'

Windy Dryden: That's what you call the level of adjustment, isn't it?

John Rowan: Yes. I regard people like that as having horizons that are too low. But they are entitled to that as long as they don't say there *is* nothing else.

Windy Dryden: Right. Now let's have a look at psychotherapy provision in the National Health Service. It seems to me that given the money available, you are bound to go the route of adjustment in that area, aren't you?

John Rowan: I don't know. You see, I think that there is increasing awareness now of counselling and therapy. There's hardly a radio programme where the person on the end of the microphone doesn't say something like, 'I think what you need is to go to Relate. If you just hold on, my assistant will give you the number to ring, or the address to write to'. It seems really common now for people to take on board that counselling or therapy might be a good thing. I think it is growing.

Windy Dryden: I don't dispute that, but what I am saying is that the NHS can't provide it.

John Rowan: No, well, I think this is the question of people paying for it, and I think that is something which people are gradually coming around to and realising that it is a matter of priorities. It doesn't cost any more than it does to buy a lot of magazines or lots of drink or cigarettes, or lots of cinema tickets or pop concert tickets, or whatever else it is that you spend your money on. You can get quite good service for quite reasonable fees. Funnily enough, someone pointed out that it is very much in tune with the spirit of Thatcherism, of self-help and 'get on your bike'. There's a sort of paradox about that, that the sort of rather advanced ideas which I think of myself as espousing actually tie in quite well with what I would regard as the rather nasty regressive ideas of people like Margaret Thatcher.

Windy Dryden: Right. Now, finally, how does what we have spoken about today fit in with one of the most important trends within the field, which is the movement towards integrative psychotherapy?

John Rowan: Well, I think that is very much in favour of what I am saying. The whole idea of integration in psychotheapy, it seems to me, is that either you do the whole job or at least you know who does. At least you know what the complementary facilities are that you are not offering. And I think that is an admirable movement which I am entirely in favour of.
    The other movement which is very popular, which is what I am not so much in favour of, is the movement towards short-term therapy. I think as soon as you go in for brief therapy bound by particular symptoms and a particular contract, and so forth, you are bound to stay at a level of

adjustment. You're bound to sell the person short on the possible initiation that's being opened up for them by their current crisis.

Windy Dryden: But playing devil's advocate for the moment, how would you respond to the argument that most people don't want to go for all these levels? They would be quite happy to return to a prior level of adjustment. And why should they entertain anything different?

John Rowan: Well, I just see a crisis as an opportunity, particularly about the age of 30 or so, which is the sort of classic age for coming into psychotherapy. You get to the age of 30 and according to research this is quite a classic age for re-evaluating your job and your relationship, or your marriage. Now, suppose some crisis takes you into counselling or therapy at that stage. It's a great opportunity to re-evaluate your whole life and your whole set-up. And you may be fobbed off by somebody who says to you: 'Oh, this is just a minor crisis, you don't want to worry too much about it, we will soon pull you through. Six weeks will do it.' I think that is robbing the person of the opportunity to treat that as a kind of initiation into a new life, a new level of personhood. Now, the person doesn't have to take that opportunity, but if he is never offered it, it seems to me you are selling him short, you are cheating him. You are saying, 'No, I'm sorry, I'm not interested', and I think a counsellor or therapist who just isn't interested is somebody I despise.

Windy Dryden: They should get out of the field, basically?

John Rowan: I think they are so limited that I would like to call them something other than therapists. Something like 'human mechanics'. And I don't want human mechanics about the place.

Windy Dryden: Well, John, I hope you don't encounter too many of them. I think we will stop there. Thank you.

References

ELLIS, A. and YEAGER, R. (1989). *Why Some Therapies Don't Work: The Dangers of Transpersonal Psychology*. Buffalo, NY: Prometheus Books.

GLOUBERMAN, D. (1989). *Life Choices and Life Changes through Imagework*. London: Mandala.

MALAN, D. (1979). *Individual Psychotherapy and the Science of Psychodynamics*. London: Butterworths.

WALKENSTEIN, E. (1975). *Shrunk to Fit*. London: Coventure.

WILBER, K. (1986). The spectrum of development. The spectrum of psychopathology. Treatment modalities. In: K. Wilber, J. Engler and D.P. Brown (eds), *Transformations of Consciousness*. Boston: New Science Library.

Chapter 11
Spirituality and the Person-centred Counsellor
An Interview with Brian Thorne

In one of his most recent books, Brian Thorne describes a mystical experience which he had at the age of nine and which proved to have a decisive influence on his subsequent development (Thorne, 1991). In essence this experience gave him glimpses of the infinite value of the human person in the eyes of God. It is this basic conviction which, despite many theological tensions and institutional frustrations, has enabled him to remain in membership of the Anglican Church from childhood until the present day. It has also underpinned his professional life as a person-centred counsellor for over 20 years.

Brian began his career as a schoolmaster after a degree in modern languages from Cambridge and teacher training at Bristol University where he was much influenced by the pioneering efforts of Elizabeth Richardson who brought the study of group dynamics and the work of the Tavistock Institute into the classroom. At Eastbourne College (1962–67), where he taught 'A' level French and German, he quickly became involved in pastoral work with many troubled adolescents and as a direct outcome he came to know George Lyward, the distinguished founder of Finchden Manor, a therapeutic community for boys and young men. He was among the first students in Britain to undertake professional training as a counsellor (at Reading University) and studied under Bruce Shertzer of Purdue University who introduced him to client-centred therapy and the work of Carl Rogers with whom he was later to form an important friendship. From 1968 to 1973 there followed a spell as a counsellor at Keele University under the pioneering leadership of Audrey Newsome and in 1974 he moved to the University of East Anglia in Norwich as the founding Director of a new Counselling Service.

Brian has remained in Norwich ever since where, in addition to his work at the University, he has also co-founded the Norwich Centre, Britain's first counselling agency committed to the person-centred approach, and helped to establish, through his co-directorship of the Facilitator Development Institute (recently re-named Person-Centred Therapy, Britain), the primary training course for person-centred therapists in the United Kingdom. With PCT co-director Dave Mearns of Jordanhill College, he wrote *Person-centred Counselling in Action* in 1988 and this book has proved to be one of the most influential texts (and the best-selling) in Britain today.

Throughout his 23 years as a person-centred therapist, Brian has been concerned to relate his theological and psychological understanding of experience and this has, at times, led to a somewhat lonely position both within the international person-centred community and within the Church. In recent years, however, and especially since Rogers' death in 1987, his theory and practice have gained a wider acceptance both among fellow professionals and in Church circles. In the interview which follows there are several moments when the counsellor and the liberal churchman unite in the exploration of spiritual experience which has increasingly become for Brian the context where the therapeutic relationship gives rise to the most fascinating discoveries.

Windy Dryden: In this interview, Brian, I want to explore with you the relationship between the spiritual dimension and counselling. But first, perhaps you could explain what *you* mean by the word 'spirituality'?

Brian Thorne: Yes. I think that in order to do that I would need to say something about what I understand to be the core of the personality, the 'self', if you like, at its deepest level. I see that core, in my own terminology, as the *spirit* of the person, as the human spirit. Now, what I mean by spirituality is really the whole process of discovering that essential self, discovering that spirit within, and then launching out on what seems to me almost an inevitable journey, once that discovery has been made. So for me spirituality is the discovery of the human spirit and then the journey which ensues once that discovery has been made in some way. That core of the personality, the human spirit when it is discovered, when it is touched, enables the human being to be open to experience in quite new and important ways which previously would not have been possible until that depth had been achieved. Use the phrase, if you like, 'open to the transcendent' – open to a whole range of experience which previously would have been denied.

Windy Dryden: Right. Now, as a dyed-in-the-wool atheist, I must ask you if you are not just replacing the phrase 'core self' with the term 'spirit'? Would that be fair?

Brian Thorne: I think in many ways it *would* be fair, yes. But then in turn I would have to ask you, dyed-in-the-wool atheist that you are, what you understand by that notion of the self. But I think I am actually using the term 'human spirit' as my understanding of the self at the deepest level.

Windy Dryden: So for you, then, the spiritual dimension doesn't have to be equated with the religious dimension of human life.

Brian Thorne: No, it doesn't. I think for me there is a distinction to be made between religion and spirituality. Religion, for me, is a formalised, often institutionalised, way of thinking about and responding to the spiritual dimension. It is in many ways the exterior form given to this interior reality. But I don't myself believe that it is in the least important for a person to be religious in that sense in order to be fully in touch with their own spiritual being.

Windy Dryden: Would you say that at present the work that is being done in the spiritual dimension of counselling really does touch the religious dimension? You were speaking earlier about being 'open to the transcendent', which means to me being more than just open to experience: it's being open to an experience of a special type, if you like a mystical, transcendent or transpersonal type. I wonder if you would like to comment on that?

Brian Thorne: Yes. It seems to me that clearly an individual person may be in touch at different times with what we might call the transcendent.

Windy Dryden: By which you mean?

Brian Thorne: By which I mean experience beyond that which the individual in his or her normal, rational, day-to-day life might be led to expect. That's a rather long-winded expression, but it is something which goes beyond the ordinary capacities of the rational ego. I could say more on that if you wanted, but that will do for the moment. The point I was going to make is that it seems to me that an individual may apprehend the transcendental in all sorts of ways, and will then clearly be struggling to make some kind of sense of the experience. Very often it seems to me that a person may have an experience that falls into this kind of category, which is actually very distressing and disturbing. It may even make a person wonder if he or she is going off his or her head. It may of course produce a sense of sublime ecstasy, but whatever it is, it's likely to cause some kind of disorientation. Now what I see at the moment is quite a number of people within counselling situations struggling with experiences of one sort or another which they don't quite know what to do with. They don't know what labels to stick on them. All they know is that they are important in some way, and may be distressing in other ways, yet usually through total ignorance, they make no reference to the whole corpus of knowledge about such experiences which is enshrined in some of the great world religions. It is almost as if individuals are re-inventing the wheel and not finding that very easy to do, because they either have no contact with what for the moment we will call institutionalised religion, or they have had some unfortunate contact with it and as a result have totally rejected it.

Windy Dryden: Right. Perhaps we could make this a little more concrete by talking about work that you have done with such a person.

Brian Thorne: Yes. I think for the person-centred practitioner, the most common route to this spiritual core is through the relationship which develops between the counsellor and client. To put it in a person-centred framework, where a client is truly receptive and responsive to the core conditions, feels genuinely accepted and understood, and believes himself to be with somebody who is not manipulating him in some way, then there is a quality of experiencing which often (and I would use the word 'often') triggers the client into a new arena of experience. It catches him often by surprise. There is a sense of being in the presence of forces, usually benevolent forces, which gives him a renewed sense of his own strength and capacity. They are forces, if you like, that breed hopefulness. People find it really quite difficult to talk about such experiences with clarity; all they know is that they seem to be in touch with something that transcends the interaction which is going on between them and their counsellor, and they will eventually, if not at the time itself, begin to comment on it and to explore it. Now that's the sort of experience that as a therapist I would want to make possible for my client and then to offer a context for making sense of it.

Windy Dryden: But you see what I find puzzling in that description is that if we look at the writings of Carl Rogers, he would say something like this: 'Yes, the person as a result of a therapeutic relationship will in a sense be able – outside of his or her awareness – to get in touch with denied experiences which are positive; but we don't have to use terms like "the transcendent" and "the spiritual" to explain these things, they can be explained within the language of psychology.' So I ask why we have to use terms like 'spiritual' and 'transcendent' for experiences which Carl Rogers adequately explained within a psychological domain.

Brian Thorne: I would question whether he did adequately explain them and I don't think he himself would have claimed that he did. If you look at some of his writing shortly before he died, he is actually struggling quite hard to give some shape to these experiences. He is himself using words like 'spiritual', 'mystical' and 'transcendental', and ackowledging that in the past he has not given them the kind of credence and depth of exploration that they deserve. I think what we actually see in Rogers is somebody who, towards the end of his life, was having to acknowledge a whole area of experience which he was also humble enough to admit that he didn't as yet fully understand. But he realised that it was significant and needed to be taken on board, although I think that I would question whether he himself would have explained this in psychological terms. But to answer your question more broadly, it seems to me that you have to ask what is meant by a 'psychological framework'. What does a psychological framework contain? What are admissible data for a psychological framework and what are inadmissible data? Rightly or wrongly I tend to see a psychological framework as somewhat constraining. It doesn't allow for experiences that actually take us beyond our normal day-to-day interactions, even if it can just about cope with extremely unusual day-to-day interactions.

Windy Dryden: I don't question at all the idea that humans can have experiences that they can't explain by their present state of knowledge, but why do we have to call these experiences spiritual, transcendental or transpersonal? Why not acknowledge that throughout the history of time, humans have had experiences that they haven't been able to explain, which later on they *could* explain?

Brian Thorne: Well, we are in danger here of going round in a complete circle, but I think it's an interesting circle nonetheless. I would certainly be prepared to accept that the words I am using, like 'transcendental' and 'spiritual' and all the rest, are simply words which are temporarily convenient to employ. They are useful because, for me, anyway, they enable me to describe my reality more effectively. I am, however, quite happy to believe that the day will come when in fact we *shall* understand all these things. Indeed, that is, if I may say so, implicit in *Christian* belief, namely that the day will come when all shall be revealed. It may not be revealed in this life – it may be revealed in the life of the spirit beyond death, but ultimately all *shall* be revealed. So I think my response to you would be: 'OK, if you don't like these words, I am quite happy for you to say that we only, as yet, have a grasp of a small part of reality; there is a great deal more for us to discover, and let's get on with it.' I am content with that idea, because it in no way refutes my underpinning belief that the essential reality is in fact a spiritual reality. Is that a fair rejoinder?

Windy Dryden: Yes. Now, moving away from that – how does this spiritual dimension, broadly speaking, affect the counselling relationship?

Brian Thorne: Well, I think it can affect it in a number of ways. I have already alluded to one, which I think is fairly often experienced by people as a totally unexpected one. This is the touching of a greater depth within the personality, through the nature of the counselling relationship. It is the relationship which gives access to it. I think this is a most exciting way in which the spiritual dimension develops through the counselling relationship. There are other instances, though (and this seems to me to be increasingly the case), where people present themselves to counsellors and therapists, almost saying in their first breath, 'I have a spiritual concern or issue that I need to tackle'. Incidentally, I think that is a very significant development; I don't remember people saying that to me 10 or 15 years ago. But now it seems to me that it is not uncommon, even in universities, with young people who clearly have had very little contact with anything that you might call institutionalised religion. I think, too, that when people have fallen foul of relationships in major ways and have been put in touch with quite intolerable pain, it is precisely the pain which can open the path to spiritual experience.

Windy Dryden: But wouldn't those same people, say about 10 or 15 years ago, have come to counselling saying, 'I have an *existential* concern'? I mean, in a way, aren't they saying, 'I really want to look at my place in the world and begin questioning the meaning that I have in myself and the world; I want to explore that'? Are they, in your terms, saying more than that? Is the spiritual dimension more than an existential one that is concerned with meaning as I have outlined it?

Brian Thorne: It is certainly concerned with meaning. I will accept that. Yes, I think a person who comes and says 'I have a spiritual concern', is perhaps almost inevitably grappling with issues of value and meaning. But I think what may differentiate the people I am talking about, those likely to arrive on the doorstep today, from the ones who came a decade ago, is that they are actually wanting and willing to consider meaning and value in a very much broader kind of context. They are open to the possibility of infinite varieties of experience in a way which I think many people some years ago were not. Or they would have been extraordinarily cautious or suspicious about them, and if a counsellor in any way seemed to be encouraging or facilitating such experiences, they might well have become very resistant.

Perhaps I might just add a personal word here, which I think is quite important. Ten years or so ago I think many of my clients, when they discovered, as they invariably did, that I had a religious commitment (that I wasn't just, as it were, 'into spirituality' but I was old-fashioned enough still to belong to an institutional church), it made them extremely uneasy. Very often I recall having to thrash the issue through with clients and to assure them that in no way was my religious affiliation going to be an impediment between us. Now I find that there are actually quite a number of clients who come to me specifically because I have a religious allegiance, and that's not because they want to be Christians. They have no sense of wanting to join a church or anything like that, but they sense that I have some kind of valid experience in this area which somehow has significance for them.

Windy Dryden: Right. I understand, Brian, that you are perhaps unique within the person-centred therapeutic world in that you have become quite interested in what is known as intrauterine experience. I wonder, since that is falling within your definition of the spiritual, if you could say a little bit more about that experience and how you have encountered it in your counselling relationships.

Brian Thorne: Yes, this is extraordinarily interesting and has become very important for me. It happened quite by accident, if that's the right way of putting it. What I mean is this: that there was a client, and subsequently there have been others, where the quality of the relationship was such that without any kind of incitement or inducement on my part (as far as I am aware) the client began to get in touch with experience which was initially very puzzling, very bewildering, and in fact acutely painful. Now, when I say the quality of the relationship was such, that seems to me to be enormously significant. I was talking earlier about the relationship itself giving access to unusual and often painful experiences, and there are undoubtedly some which if we have the courage to stay with, gradually become focused on pre-birth memories. For me this was extraordinarily mysterious to start with; also, I must confess, somewhat frightening. That fear has now gone. I am absolutely convinced of the reality of intrauterine experience.

Windy Dryden: Perhaps you could shed some light on a doubting Thomas over here.

Brian Thorne: When I say I am absolutely convinced, I mean that I have been alongside people whose experience clearly points to such an extraordinary sense of threat or annihilation or hostility of a major order, that one gradually intuits that this was something which was happening to them before they were born. They may have no consciousness of it, but it is being relived within the therapeutic relationship. Now, when I say I am convinced, I mean first that some of the experiences that people have undergone with me I can find no other explanation for. Secondly, and more importantly for the doubting Thomas sitting over there, on those occasions where it has actually been possible to check out with the client's mother what was going on in the pregnancy, the mother's evidence has been wholly confirmatory. For example, the mother admits: 'Yes, it is true that I tried to abort you.' 'Yes, it is true that I was deeply grieving during the first months of my pregnancy.' Whatever it may be, the mother produces, as it were, the objective evidence, which is wholly confirmatory of the extraordinary experience which the client has undergone with me. I don't call this primal work, in any conventional sense, because as I say, we have almost stumbled on it by accident – but it has happened. Such experiences raise fundamental questions such as who is the person in the womb who is experiencing this? Do I simply think in terms of the fetus – the fetus at the age of two months, or three weeks, or whatever? I prefer, myself, the hypothesis of 'the spirit'; that this being at the deepest level of his or her reality is already very much open to pain, to the threat of annihilation, and is experiencing everything at the deepest possible level; which also leads me to feel that the human spirit might well have existed before birth.

Windy Dryden: Well, I was going to go on to that, strangely enough, because I guess that once you open yourself up to experiences that initially you find very puzzling, that you begin to recognise, yes, those things are possible, then the next step would be to open yourself up to experiences which, earlier on in your development as a counsellor, you would have found too bizarre to be true. For example, some of the fringe therapies like 'reincarnation therapy' may indeed be questionable, but I think this is an area that we are beginning to talk about. What is the origin of the spirit? Could not that spirit have been alive in other bodies? This is the area which I think we are talking about.

Brian Thorne: I think it is, yes, and as far as I am concerned I detect in myself an openness to some of these hypotheses that was certainly not in me, say, 10 years ago. I think I have become increasingly convinced that the deepest reality is the spiritual reality, and therefore I have to ask precisely the questions that you are posing there. What is spirit?

Windy Dryden: Well, to my mind it is clearly far more than 'self', as we discussed earlier.

Brian Thorne: Yes, and I think what is interesting in the therapeutic context is that so very often when a person is in touch with this 'spiritual self' (or what you will), he or she is usually conscious at one and the same time of individual uniqueness and of interconnectedness with others, and often too with the whole created order. Now that seems to me to be a very extraordinary thing, to be simultaneously experiencing personal uniqueness and a kind of connectedness or corporate identity, or whatever you may like to call it. But that again rings a lot of bells in terms of various theological doctrines from many of the world religions and certainly it is there in Christianity.

Windy Dryden: Do these experiences that you have encountered clinically lead you to find the confines of person-centred therapy in some ways constraining?

Brian Thorne: In some ways, yes, Windy. But in other ways, no. By that I mean that any kind of theoretical construct must have its shortcomings; by definition every theory is temporary, isn't it? Rogers himself (and I find this very reassuring) maintained that there was only one thing that you could be sure about in any theory, and that is that there were mistakes in it; or that it was in fact inadequate and would have to be modified and redefined. And I suppose why I don't find the person-centred practice too confining, is because of the emphasis, which has been there from the beginning, on openness to experience. Essentially person-centred therapy is based on the trustworthiness of experiencing, and therefore if what is actually being experienced by a client (or more likely client and counsellor together) is truely trustworthy, then let's stay with it and see where we go. I suppose in the last years of Rogers' life there is a great deal of evidence that he too was beginning to trust forms of experience which he had previously not trusted.

Windy Dryden: Do you encounter within the person-centred tradition much bewilderment regarding these ideas when you talk about them within that community?

Brian Thorne: Yes, I do.

Windy Dryden: Could you say a little more about that?

Brian Thorne: Yes, certainly. It would be simplistic to say that person-centred therapists divide into two camps, but it sometimes feels like that to me. When I do speak about these matters, or write about them, I tend to get, on the one hand, those who are fully responsive and very enthusiastic about what I am saying; they actually say, 'Yes, I know about that, that's what has been going on for me too, and it's an inevitable development from the person-centred trust in experiencing'. But, on the other hand, there are others who tend to say that I am colluding with the worst in Rogers, that I am colluding with what happened to the old man when he was getting pretty gaga, and was obviously very conscious of his own mortality. These people say that I and my ilk are doing the whole person-centred tradition a gross disservice, because it's difficult enough anyway for person-centred practitioners to hold up their heads with honour among the cognitive–behaviourists and the analytic folk; and if we start getting into all this weird spiritual stuff, then we shall really find ourselves firmly at the bottom of the league.

Windy Dryden: So what they are saying is that you may be going a little gaga yourself, along with Carl at the end of his days. But also, if you are going to talk about this, keep it quiet because if it comes out into the professional community we'll be the laughing stock.

Brian Thorne: Yes, I think there are people who really do feel that and believe it quite passionately, and to whom I am not a very popular figure to have around. I think what makes me, in a way, rather peculiar too, is that my Christian commitment and my theological understandings actually preceded my person-centred understanding of reality.

Windy Dryden: I think I prefer the word 'unique' there, instead of 'peculiar', Brian. We are talking about going gaga, but I take your point.

Brian Thorne: I suppose that where I am to some extent perhaps winning back a little respectability among these people is that they see me now trying to make sense of clinical experience in theological terms. They may not like the notion of theological terms, but at least the marriage between psychology and theology is a more respectable and admirable thing to be doing than simply hiving off into a kind of individualistic, transcendental trip.

Windy Dryden: Right. So if you were to respond to your critics within the person-centred tradition, what would you say to them in terms of your ideas in this realm?

Brian Thorne: I would say to them something like this: don't feel that this kind of work is actually discreditable; on the contrary, look at what is happening globally to the understanding of reality and you will find in many cultures, and in many different parts of the world, a new openness to understanding experience beyond the confines of the materialistic world we inhabit. We are actually in the vanguard, and the very fact that clients are increasingly presenting themselves saying that this in some mysterious way is of relevance and importance to them, should be signal enough that we are not actually moving off into some really rather disreputable cul de sac. We are actually grappling with what seem to be, increasingly, issues that confront us not only as individuals but as a global community.

Windy Dryden: Now elsewhere in this book, Brian, John Rowan makes the point that in order to work with the whole human being, counsellors and therapists really need to be open to a wide number of realms, and he includes the spiritual. His point is this, that if you don't accept or open yourself up to these experiences, in a sense you are going to be doing the individual that you are facing a great disservice. You are going to be offering them less than optimal counselling. Would you go along with that point of view? Does that logically follow what we have been discussing today?

Brian Thorne: I suppose it follows in a way, but it seems to me to be a bit harsh. It's almost like a recipe for perfection in the therapeutic profession, which would have about it, as far as I am concerned, its own dangers. I think we might arrive at a situation where therapists were feeling that they must somehow be open to spiritual reality and therefore they had better get themselves, in some curious way, retrained, or whatever.

Windy Dryden: Or trainers will only be accepting people on to their training courses if they have had such experiences.

Brian Thorne: Yes. And I would feel that that is actually not a recipe for perfection, but a recipe for disaster, because there is nothing worse than what we might call pseudo-spiritual experiencing; and the notion that somehow therapists have to get themselves keyed up spiritually in order to do the job properly sends shivers down my spine. I would much prefer therapists to be working in those areas and with that kind of material about which they feel capable, confident, and all the rest of it, than to be embarking on a spiritual journey simply because they feel they ought to.

Windy Dryden: And yet there is in what you are saying the idea that such therapists or counsellors who are not open to that spiritual realm do have limitations. They are not going to be able to facilitate a relationship in which intrauterine experiences will be identified. They won't be able to enable a client to really explore experiences that are beyond *their* comprehension.

Brian Thorne: Well, let's wait a minute. Because as I was saying a few minutes ago, my own initial experiences of working with people in the intrauterine arena happened fortuitously, and not by design. It happened because of the nature of the relationship which I actually was able to create with my client. Therefore I suppose what I am really trying to say there is that what matters is not so much therapists' understanding of spirituality, or their hypotheses about the nature of that spiritual reality, but their preparedness to be open to experience and to offer their clients a relationship which is actually truly acceptant and understanding.

Windy Dryden: OK, I take that point, but clearly if counsellors regard that whole realm as poppycock, then they would not be able to facilitate a relationship where those experiences would be able to become identified and symbolised as such.

Brian Thorne: I suppose if somebody regards something as poppycock, that means that they are going to be totally resistant to any experience which might fall into that area. That's what you are saying, isn't it? I suppose I would have to acknowledge that that might well be the case. But I think among many therapists I know, there are all sorts of developing perceptions. There is increasingly a willingness to be open to new understandings of reality. Getting back to what you were saying just now, simply the notion that we only know the half of it, or the quarter of it, seems to me to be a fairly common attitude not only among therapists, but indeed among a lot of thinking people nowadays. And that preparedness to acknowledge that we don't actually know (a humility, if you like, before human experience, and therefore before the therapeutic encounter) seems to me to be what is really essential in the therapist. In fact, I may go a little bit further. It seems to me that one of the things that can happen is that somebody who is apparently spiritually very sophisticated, who has all sorts of interesting hypotheses about spiritual reality, can actually be an impediment to the client's exploration.

Windy Dryden: Because they would be too quick to symbolise that experience as within that realm.

Brian Thorne: Absolutely.

Windy Dryden: So what you seem to be saying is that what is more important in a way than actual experience of the spiritual dimension in oneself as a counsellor, is an openness to experience, but an openness to experience that is wider, in fact much wider than what appears in the writings of Carl Rogers, and particularly in his heyday.

Brian Thorne: Yes, I think that is true. I think I would have to accept that, and yet at the same time, as I said earlier, it seems to me within the core of Rogers' work right from the outset there was always this deep respect for the client's experience, a deep respect for subjective reality. And if a client therefore is actually bringing to the counsellor a subjective reality which impinges upon the spiritual dimension, it would seem to me that the person-centred therapist has no option but to go along with that, to be as committed a companion as he can be.

Windy Dryden: I think that is a good place to end.

References

MEARNS, D. and THORNE, B.J. (1988). *Person-centred Counselling in Action*. London: Sage.

THORNE, B.J. (1991). *Behold the Man*. London: Darton, Longman & Todd.

Chapter 12
Growing Together
An Interview with John and Marcia Davis

Although they were born on opposite sides of the Atlantic, John and Marcia Davis shared an East European Jewish ancestry, childhoods spent in the suburbs of a large metropolis (John in London, Marcia in New York), female-dominated families that included resident maternal grandmothers and the breaking of new family ground in attending university.

John's fondest childhood memories are of his time at boarding-school in the country, to which he and his sister were evacuated following the London blitz. His first loves were chess, music, languages and mathematics. He left school early after gaining an Open Scholarship in Mathematics at New College, Oxford, and during his military service trained as a Russian translator. At Oxford he took first degrees in mathematics and in psychology and philosophy (PPP), but was better known for his punting and his parties than for his scholarship. A search for new horizons took him, improbably, to Bloomington, Indiana, on a Fulbright travel scholarship, where he eventually enrolled in the Indiana University clinical psychology doctoral programme.

Marcia grew up in the street culture of Brooklyn, a regular member of the gang, an honours stream student in a high school of 5000 pupils, and an example to her two younger sisters. An asthmatic child, she was prescribed long annual vacations in the Catskills, a storehouse of idyllic memories. A New York State Scholarship enabled her to attend Barnard College where she majored in psychology, but also studied Russian to indulge her literary interests. She was, and remains, a keen dancer. A desire for adventure and the offer of an assistantship persuaded her to go to graduate school in Indiana, where she soon transferred to the clinical psychology doctoral programme. Kindred spirits in the wilderness, she and John eventually married and started a family. Classroom lactation notwithstanding, they continued their training uninterrupted.

They interned together in San Francisco at the then Langley Porter Neuropsychiatric Institute, coming to England on completion of their doctorates. Since that time Marcia has worked primarily in the National Health Service, in Oxford, Sheffield, Doncaster and Coventry, where she is currently District Clinical Psychologist; she is also part-time Senior Lecturer in the Department of Psychology at the University of Warwick. John has held academic appointments at Oxford Polytechnic, Sheffield University and Warwick University, where he is currently Senior Lecturer in the Department of Psychology; he also works sessionally in the National Health Service in Coventry, where he is Consultant Clinical Psychologist with special responsibility for dissociative disorders. John and Marcia together run the MSc course in Psychotherapy at Warwick University and are engaged together in research on the development of psychotherapists, on therapists' difficulties and coping strategies, and on the epidemiology of dissociative disorders. Their developing work with dissociative problems has made Coventry one of the few centres in Britain with experience in the therapy of multiple personality and ritually abused adults. In the interview that follows it will become clear how this line of work has resonated with their life as a married couple.

Windy Dryden: John and Marcia, you have been married for 28 years and throughout that time you have both worked as psychotherapists. In this interview I want to consider the relationship between your being married and your work as psychotherapists. So perhaps we could start with the first question. What would you say was the most important issue to come out of the relationship between being married and being psychotherapists?

John Davis: I think there are two important issues, of which I would say one is more important. One issue has to do with drawing the boundaries between our private life as a married couple, and our professional lives as therapists working with clients. The second issue has to do with the breadth or narrowness of the private lives we lead in relation to our practice as therapists. They seem to me to be the two important issues.

Windy Dryden: Marcia?

Marcia Davis: Yes, I would go along with what John has said. I was thinking as he was talking about that, whether in some sense that issue is also an individual issue. I think each individual has decisions to make about the breadth and narrowness of his or her personal life. I think for me another issue, personally, is the amount of support that has been given to me both in my married life and in my personal and professional life – whether in some senses that is again restrictive or enhancing.

Windy Dryden: OK. Let's start off with the issue of the placing of boundaries between the professional and personal aspects of your lives together. When you think of that issue, what immediately comes to mind?

John Davis: Well, I think one thing that comes to mind in the first place, certainly for me (and Marcia might want to comment on this from her point of view) is that the kind of therapeutic work I have been doing has changed over the years. In more recent years, the last 10 or 15 years, I think I have been working much more intensively with a different kind of population of clients with different kinds of problems. That has really brought these kinds of questions into prominence because I have been very immersed in this work as a therapist, and before that I don't think therapeutic work seemed to impinge very much on our married life. But in more recent years it's had the potential to do that.

Windy Dryden: In what way?

John Davis: Well, in that I have felt the need to devote a lot of time, energy and personal investment in the therapeutic work that I have been doing, and I have therefore had sometimes less time, space and energy to invest in our private life together. So that has required finding the right balance.

Windy Dryden: What impact has John's work in this area had on you, Marcia, in terms of your relationship together?

Marcia Davis: I think it has gone through stages, Windy. I think in the earlier stages I was quite resentful of that at times, and really felt it was taking over John's life. I think that was resolved to some degree by John. But in addition, as my own work has moved on, and as our family commitments have altered too, I have also got involved with certain very demanding kinds of cases – demanding because of the nature of the issues involved. It's meant that I have got much more caught up, in a similar way to John.

Windy Dryden: In terms of time?

Marcia Davis: Yes, in terms of the time, the demands, the abnormal working hours, the days, evenings and weekends; and I have really been able to look back and understand the kind of dilemmas that John must have felt at that time, and the difficulties for him. It's made me very appreciative of the support that he has been able to give me. It still raises questions for me, and perhaps for both of us, as to what the boundary is and should be between professional and personal lives. Getting the balance right as to how much time to devote to each of these does seem to be a problem.

Windy Dryden: In what ways is it a problem currently?

Marcia Davis: I think that currently (and I hesitate to speak for both of us, but we have talked quite a bit about this) there is a sense that professional matters can take over our lives completely. Most of our relationships, I think, are now with other people in the same 'business', if you like, and it feels that we have fewer personal friendships, and we have relationships which are friendly but tend to be work-related. That has felt restrictive. I had never intended to get so involved professionally. Now I see quite considerable gaps occurring by not having kept up our friendships. But there has been very little time and space for that.

Windy Dryden: So would it be fair to say that the boundary issue in a way caused the other issue that John raised initially, which was how broadly or narrowly do you live your lives?

Marcia Davis: Yes, exactly. Because we are both very much in the same field and even within that many of our concerns have become very similar, particularly recently. There is less to be brought in from elsewhere, from other contacts, other hobbies, that sort of thing.

John Davis: I don't really agree with that entirely. I think that they are somewhat separate issues. I don't think the boundary issues are quite the same as the issues to do with breadth and narrowness of external relationships. There is a link between those things, it seems to me, which has to do with a particular kind of therapeutic work that we are more recently involved in, and I think that the effect of that is almost to set us aside from people who have very little awareness of the kinds of issues that we work with, and also the kinds of worlds that our clients are showing to us. And it is much easier to have relationships with people who have some inkling about these things.

Windy Dryden: I think at this point the reader might be more than a little curious about what types of clients we are referring to here. So perhaps you could make that clearer.

John Davis: Well, in recent years both of us have done a great deal of work with people who have been sexually abused as children and who have led very traumatic existences; with people who have multiple personalities; and with people who have been ritually abused in cults. And that has opened our eyes to worlds which previously we had not been at all familiar with.

Windy Dryden: There's a sense, in terms of what you were saying earlier, that this work has led you both to feel distant from other professional colleagues, who don't work with such clients.

John Davis: Yes, I think that's true. There is a growing awareness within the professional field of these kinds of issues and problems, and to some extent we play the part of publicising them, and drawing attention to them within the professional field. But I think it is still the case that people who lack any experience of working in these kinds of areas are set aside in some way and don't quite inhabit the same territory we are currently inhabiting.

Marcia Davis: I think there are also therapeutic issues about wanting to protect other people from some of the horrors that we have been exposed to. Perhaps, too, you often realise that people do not want to hear about it, either. I am just reading a book by Robert Mayer about ritual abuse, called *Satan's Children*, and he describes experiences of his own that rang bells for me about not being the best of dinner guests. There were things I was learning about ritual abuse that don't exactly make great dinner-time conversation.

Windy Dryden: Has the fact that you are both working with people who have been so traumatised led you to be much more supportive of one another?

Marcia Davis: Well, in a general way John has always been supportive of me! I am not sure I am always so supportive of him. He is always rushing off, and I really wish he was staying home. But in this connection it has, certainly for me, been helpful to have John's expertise and support to draw on. The work is very, very difficult. There is relatively little support one could gain from one's professional colleagues in an area of so little knowledge, and so little talked about.

Windy Dryden: So you feel that John is very supportive in the work you do.

Marcia Davis: Yes, I do.

Windy Dryden: Do you feel equally supported by Marcia in your work?

John Davis: Yes, I do feel supported. I feel I can unload if I need to unload. I feel that we have had another bond through sharing this line of work to add to the other things that bond us together. I also feel that in some ways, in recent years, I have modified my own therapeutic work to some extent. That's to do with the boundary issue again, and there's less tension about these issues between us, perhaps because there wasn't a clear boundary before.

Windy Dryden: Now, my understanding of working with the clients we are discussing is that there is a very sensitive issue concerning with whom one discusses the issues that crop up in such work. I understand, for example, John, that one or two of your clients even specify that you don't talk about their therapy with Marcia. Does that bring about its own strains for you both?

John Davis: Well, I feel I have quite a good understanding with the people I work with about whether they are comfortable or not with my sharing what they say with Marcia. (You will understand, by the way, that in a small community like our's my clients will know who Marcia is.) Some of the people who I work with might, as you just mentioned, say to me, 'I would like you not to talk about this with your wife', and I respect that.

Marcia Davis: Well, until today that wasn't something I particularly knew, so that's news to me. It's certainly something we haven't really discussed.

Windy Dryden: How does it feel to learn that?

Marcia Davis: Well, I think it reflects a slightly different approach that John and I might have. I don't think I would accept that kind of arrangement with my clients generally. I feel that they would need to respect my own need, or any therapist's need, for consultation or supervision, and respect my choices of individuals who might be taking on that role with me. In the case of John's clients it would be interesting to know whether the requests concern me as his wife or me as another professional. I think that is something we might talk about at some point.

Windy Dryden: Now, John, I understand that the majority of the clients with whom you work so intensively and who are so demanding of your therapeutic time are in fact women. I wondered what impact that fact has had and currently has on your relationship with one another.

John Davis: Well, I don't experience it as an issue for myself, but in a way I think that's something you would do better to ask Marcia about. Relatively few men who share these kinds of experiences have, if you like, 'come out' with them, I think, in the client role. So most people working in this kind of area are dealing with women clients.

Windy Dryden: Has that been an issue for you, Marcia?

Marcia Davis: Yes, I think in the past that was an issue at times. I felt resentful at the time, but also jealousy came into it. It was hard for a time to sort it out, how much of that was purely to do with my personal reactions and material, and whether some of that was actually emanating from the transferential and countertransferential relationships John had with some of his clients at that time, and it's something we did talk about. Those things are always quite hard to tease out but I think that was quite helpful for both of us to talk about.

Windy Dryden: Did it test your level of trust in John as a husband?

Marcia Davis: I don't think it tested my level of trust, in that I would never have thought that John would behave in any way unprofessionally. But I think it tested rather more a sense of allegiance. Did I come first, or did his clients come first? And obviously, in the end, I felt that I had to be the one, or wanted to be the one, who came first.

Windy Dryden: We discussed earlier that John made some modifications in his work with this client group. Was this a result of discussions about who came first?

Marcia Davis: Yes, I would think it did come from such discussions, and obviously from John doing a lot of thinking about things for himself, and making his own decisions about them. Is that right, John? You never know quite how decisions are reached but I am sure that was around and we did talk about it.

Windy Dryden: You are giving a wry smile, John.

John Davis: Well, I think it was quite difficult for me to accommodate to what was the problem for us in this respect and in some ways it was quite painful for me to bring about changes in the way I was working therapeutically, but I felt the need to do that and I did it. And the consequences have had to be dealt with in the therapies I was involved in.

Windy Dryden: That was at a time when you weren't both working with similar clients, I understand.

Marcia Davis: That's true.

Windy Dryden: Do you think that this issue of allegiance would crop up now, given the fact that you are both working with clients who make similar demands on you?

Marcia Davis: Well, it is difficult to take things out of their timeframe and move them forward, but on balance I would say yes. Perhaps to a, much lesser degree, but yes, I think so. I think maybe it reflects something John and I have talked about. John said to me at some point that perhaps if he hadn't got married, or wasn't married and had no family commitments, that he might have devoted himself full-time to therapeutic work, in a very intense way. I think that reflects a difference between us as individuals, because that's something I could never do. I need to have a personal life, things that are separate from my work. My work, for me, is partly a vocation, but not entirely.

Windy Dryden: One of the dynamics of this interview that won't come across is that we have several times shut the tape-recorder off to discuss the appropriateness of what we are discussing. So, perhaps having mentioned that as a dynamic, can I put it to you that we are struggling with the issue of how much of the inner workings of your relationship you want to have published and available to your clients? I sense that's a real issue at the moment.

John Davis: Yes, I think ordinarily in our private lives the things that go on are not things which I would share in therapy, even though what happens between us privately may influence things that occur in therapy. This is part of the substance of this discussion we are having. So that is one of the questions I think we need to think about together: how much of those private aspects of our married life do we want to share in an indirect way, through publicising these discussions?

Windy Dryden: Right. So I think the two themes that are coming across to me are: how much damaging impact does your work with the clients that we have been talking about have on your relationship with each other? Also, how much potential damage is there lurking about for your clients?

John Davis: Well, I think it is not necessarily, for me anyway, a question of damage to clients. It's a boundary issue, the other way round. There is more than one reason why I don't freely discuss my private married life with clients. One reason is that I owe Marcia a degree of confidentiality about what is private to us, so I don't want to breach that confidentiality without ensuring that she is comfortable about that.

Windy Dryden: I was hearing the issue a little differently. I don't know if you were, Marcia?

Marcia Davis: I think initially I was hearing perhaps more concern about the impact on your clients of knowing that I might have felt some experience of jealousy, and that I viewed it in part as a reflection of what was also happening in their therapy. That concerns less our confidentiality than the issue of the impact it might have on your clients.

John Davis: There is more than one issue.

Marcia Davis: There are both of those issues for you.

John Davis: Yes, I think that anybody who felt 'I gave John's wife cause to be jealous' might experience some distress about that and feel that they would have to deal with a sense of guilt that they had produced those feelings or had been responsible for them in some way.

Windy Dryden: It's clear to me from our discussion how important it is to keep a process view of what we are talking about. It seems that it is difficult for you to come to any clear-cut policy decision. It's as if I have been party to a discussion in which you both check out with each other what the other person means. What I am sensing is how important it is to do that if you are both working in this area and sharing it with a wider public. Having said that, perhaps we could move on to the other issue John raised, which was the issue of breadth and narrowness of your lives. Now, we have alluded to that but perhaps we could make it centre stage for a while.

Marcia Davis: I guess it's hard to tease out many different things. There's the fact that we are very close in our relationship generally, and in addition we work in the same area, and with each other. John works in my department clinically one day a week, we work in the university, teaching a course together – all this has a sense, perhaps, of excluding a lot of people from what is a very close, intimate relationship. In that sense there is something narrowing, and in other senses it is very enriching, and I think important to both of us.

Windy Dryden: But whether it's due to the work with the clients we spoke about earlier, it seems to me that the Davis field is narrowing rather than broadening.

Marcia Davis: I guess I feel there is a danger of that. It comes with many things. It may come also with an 'empty nest' quality (the family is not at home any more and so there is also a time-of-life issue). I think there's the fact, too, that we are both aware of that and talk about it, and at times make attempts to broaden out and to make sure we don't close in on each other completely. I think at the moment the kind of work we are involved in makes it hard to find a breathing space to make the efforts required to broaden out and to maintain those efforts, because it all takes time and energy. At the weekends I often feel that I haven't the energy to see anybody and a part of me would very much like to do that. But I haven't the energy to have people around to entertain them. I collapse in a heap and want somebody to do nothing but look after me for the weekend.

Windy Dryden: And perhaps you haven't the energy to be interviewed by somebody like me!

Marcia Davis: [Laughing] No, this is a pleasure, Windy.

John Davis: There are other factors here. For example, I'm relating this now to the issues we have been talking about before, the kind of work we are doing and the immersion that we have experienced in it. I think an example of an effect this has is what ordinarily or what once upon a time would have been quite attractive to me, I mean the socialising at dinner parties and the kinds of conversations that go with that, which now takes on a kind of shallow quality. In a way that kind of relating becomes less attractive because of the intensity of the gut-level relating that one is involved in in this kind of work. And that's why I think our social relationships tend to gravitate towards work-related ones, where we might be attracted to see colleagues who are engaged in similar lines of work.

Windy Dryden: So it's a different quality. For Marcia it's a question of exhaustion, that it's tiring working with such clients. There is that element there for you, John, but there is also the element of the superficiality of some of these other social relationships. I'm reminded of the joke about Albert Ellis. He was at the end of a working day, and some colleagues came round and said, 'Albert, we can do anything you want, it's up to you. Would you like to go to a show, see a movie or go dancing? What would you really like to do?'. So Albert said, 'Bring me up another client to see'. I'm picking up that sense that you really do get immersed in the intensity of that work.

John Davis: Yes, you do get immersed, I think. But the superficiality issue is not quite the same thing as the immersion. The superficiality issue has to do with operating at a very deep level of relationship in this kind of therapeutic work.

Windy Dryden: It's not the immersion per se, but the immersion at that intense level that results in you finding less time for the more superficial aspects of social relationships.

John Davis: Somehow they lose their gratification. What is the point of making polite conversation with people with whom one is not really engaging?

Marcia Davis: Can I come in? I just wanted to say that I really feel in a different place from John on that issue. I guess I feel the need for things that reflect less the dark side of people and life, a need not for superficial relationships, but relationships that have some gaiety and fun in them as much as angst and tumult.

Windy Dryden: Indeed, I want to explore the joys of being therapists in a married relationship in a minute. Before we do that, I'm wondering what effect the intensity of your work with such clients has on the intensity of your relationship with one another.

Marcia Davis: I think at one level it brings us very close because we appreciate so much more what the other has experienced, has been exposed to, has had to cope with emotionally. The other side is, of course, the exhaustion. We may want to be sitting at the dinner table reading the newspaper and not talking to each other at all.

John Davis: I don't feel that it does really colour one way or another the intensity of our relationship together. It may have transitory effects on the need for space or closeness, yes. As Marcia says, I may want to retreat to the newspaper or television sometimes. There are other times when I might want close contact. But I think in terms of the overall intensity of our relationship, that it is not very much influenced by working in this particular domain.

Windy Dryden: To conclude, let's look at the more joyful side of the relationship between being therapists and being in a marital relationship. What are those joys?

John Davis: Well, we obviously share a great deal in common, which I think is important in a close relationship. Inevitably, working in this field one is constantly examining oneself, and one's awareness of oneself is heightened. I think that makes for a deepening of relationship. It heightens the quality of relationship. I think the fact that we are both involved in this work means that there is a great deal of thought or sensitivity which goes into our relationship together, which draws on the work that we do.

Marcia Davis: I guess we both feel quite fulfilled by the work that we do in the sense that it enhances our relationship as well. It feels very important and meaningful work, and a personal satisfaction that we get from that feeds into our relationship. I think too that it has encouraged us to be more tolerant or philosophical. Perhaps we were already somewhat like that, but it has developed or enhanced a way of being with people and each other. It has enabled us to see the importance of maintaining relationships and giving individual space to each other and family, to let them be what they want to be, and to support that. It's good to have a partner who appreciates a good dream when he hears one!

John Davis: I think also the kind of therapeutic work we are involved in probably puts us very much in touch with parts of ourselves that we might not have discovered so well otherwise. There is a kind of enrichment of what we can draw on in our own relationship, and we find parts of ourselves that we maybe wouldn't have easily found otherwise. You haven't heard too much about it today, but we know how to play together too! I guess there has been a mutuality in that self-discovery.

Marcia Davis; Yes, there's a sense of growing together.

Windy Dryden: In conclusion, 'Growing together' might be a good title for our interview.